Tha's Locked Up

THA'S LOCKED UP
Memories of a West Yorkshire Policeman

David Watson

First published in Great Britain in 2012 by
Wharncliffe Books
an imprint of
Pen & Sword Books Ltd
47 Church Street
Barnsley
South Yorkshire
S70 2AS

ISBN 978-1-84884-786-6

A CIP catalogue record for this book is
available from the British Library.

Typeset in 11/1   Huddersfield, West Yorkshire

Printed and bo
CPI Group (U

Pen & Sword   & Sword
Aviation, Pen   itime,
Pen & Sword   fe Local
History, Wharncliffe True Crime, Wharncliffe Transport, Pen &
Sword Select, Pen & Sword Military Classics, Leo Cooper,
The Praetorian Press, Remember When, Seaforth Publishing
and Frontline Publishing.

For a complete list of Pen & Sword titles please contact
PEN & SWORD BOOKS LIMITED
47 Church Street, Barnsley, South Yorkshire, S70 2AS England
E-mail: enquiries@pen-and-sword.co.uk
Website: www.pen-and-sword.co.uk

Contents

Introduction   7

Chapter 1   Daylight Robbery   13
Chapter 2   Beware of the Little Green Men   25
Chapter 3   Merry Christmas   37
Chapter 4   Old Dog, New Tricks   53
Chapter 5   Miners' Strike   61
Chapter 6   Keeping Up Appearances   73
Chapter 7   Carry on Capers   79
Chapter 8   Kermit the Frog   85
Chapter 9   Testing Times   97
Chapter 10   Into Battle   105
Chapter 11   That Wise Old Cat   113
Chapter 12   Marital Bliss   121
Chapter 13   Bingo Caller   133
Chapter 14   Crazy Pursuit   141
Chapter 15   Leading by Example   153
Chapter 16   Wheelclampers   161

Epilogue   173

Introduction

'Tha's locked up', is a phrase that I have never personally used. Perhaps I should explain its significance to me. I think back to that first ever arrest. My first day at Brighouse, and I was out on patrol in a panda car with Steve, my tutor constable, when the radio message came through. A man was trying to obtain goods by deception using a stolen cheque book in one of the town's department stores. We were nearby and Steve was soon speeding towards the scene of the crime. In the meantime the thief realised that he had been rumbled and fled the scene, last seen running away along Bradford Road. 'There he is!' yelled Steve, pointing to a likely looking suspect sprinting along the crowded footpath. 'You get after him, I'll try to head him off.' He skidded to a stop and I was out of the car in an instant. Steve accelerated away in the opposite direction leaving me on my own.

There wasn't a moment to waste and within half a minute my flying rugby tackle brought the thief to a sudden stop. We both hit the deck, him landing face down on the footpath, but what now? My scrambled brain wouldn't function properly, was it adrenaline or panic or maybe a bit of both? Couldn't even remember the exact words of the police caution, or the reason for the arrest. Steve was still driving around looking for me. But help was at hand from the town centre bobby. Ray, my fellow probationer, came to help, saw me still clinging onto my prisoner as both of us lay spread-eagled on the footpath. 'As tha locked 'im up?' asked Ray. 'Erm, no, not yet,' I answered nervously. Ray prodded my prisoner with his left boot to attract his attention. 'Oye you,' he said. The thief turned to face him, 'Tha's locked up,' concluded Ray.

That was it. There was no official caution, no reason given for the arrest, just 'Tha's locked up', delivered in the broadest Yorkshire accent I'd ever heard. Those words would stay with me for a long time. Ray had just given me my first lesson on the practical way of policing the streets, even if it wasn't exactly done by the book.

Earlier, in the autumn of 1980, I had faced some difficult decisions. The building trade was in the doldrums, and as a self-employed joiner I worried about my future. Since leaving school I'd made my living in this trade. I spent four years as an apprentice before I started my own business. At first trade was good, I worked hard and there was enough profit for me to buy an old cottage on the outskirts of Bradford. My weekends were spent renovating the place until it was a charming and cosy little home. I had other commitments too, I was planning to get married and longed for a secure occupation.

One rainy afternoon I was busy making window frames in the workshop when the office phone rang, I walked through and picked up the receiver. 'Lee and Watson, plumbers and joiners, Dave Watson speaking.' It was Reginald, the architect from the construction site and today he sounded even more gloomy than usual. He wanted to know if we had been paid for our last two months work. We were one of the sub-contractors on the development of a private hospital in Leeds, and as the site agent, as well as the architect, Reginald usually knew what was going on. I didn't like the way that this conversation was heading.

'No, they've not sent a cheque yet,' I replied. 'Why, is there a problem?'

'There certainly is,' he replied, 'the other subcontractors haven't been paid for weeks, nor have I or the plasterers or the electricians and now you too. I've tried to contact Asquith's but their phone's been cut off. I've heard on the grapevine that they've gone bust, and the bloody thieves have taken our money with them.'

I was gutted and slumped down in the office chair as Reginald ranted on about the unpaid invoices. We were relying on that money to pay the trade suppliers' bills. And now we wouldn't be getting paid. Over four thousand quid down the drain. Not a great deal of money in the scheme of things, but still hard to find for a couple of self-employed tradesmen. We were in the middle of a recession and it was beginning to bite, leaving us working ourselves into the ground to keep our business afloat. The building trade was starting to get me down. Surely there was a better way to make a living, maybe it really was time to look for another job.

By October 1981 my life had changed dramatically. I jumped to attention as the red-faced drill sergent screamed, 'GEEET OOOON PARADE!'. We stood on the parade square at Bishopgarth in Wakefield, my first day as Police Constable 1021 David Watson. Dozens of feet quickly shuffled backwards and forwards, or to the left or the right, trying to get into some sort of formation.

I stood to attention, back ramrod straight, stomach pulled in and chest pushed out, arms straight down by my sides with thumbs perfectly in line with the seams of my trousers. There I stood, one of thirty-three brand new recruits sworn in as constables in the West Yorkshire Metropolitan Police Force. To hell with the building trade I thought. I'd had enough of it. I wanted a recession-proof job, and judging by the recent inner city riots, joining the boys in blue seemed to be the answer. But first I had to survive police training school.

The day kicked off in the classroom, time for a 'get to know each other' session. Each recruit was called to the front of the classroom to address our colleagues by giving a 5-minute biography about ourselves. I listened as each person stood up and gave a potted history of their life so far. After two hours I knew that eleven of my fellow recruits were former police cadets, another five were from the armed forces and a couple were straight from university. There was one former teacher, one nurse plus two or three who had previously worked in banking or insurance; and one bloke who had been a professional rugby player. I soon realised that very few of my colleagues were from manual jobs, in fact, I narrowed it down to just two, me and one other bloke who was a former truck driver.

With the introductions over it was time for the training sergeant to put the fear of god into us. More than twenty applicants for every job, he repeatedly told us, constantly reminding us how fortunate we were, before spending half an hour telling us why we could get kicked out of the Force. Dishonesty was the first reason, no problem there for me, then there was excessive use of force. Nothing to worry about there either, I didn't consider myself to be a violent or aggressive bloke. But his next subject did cause me some concern; ten per cent of all recruits were expected to lose their jobs in the first three months for failing to pass the weekly law exams at District Training School. I looked around at my new colleagues, now feeling rather anxious and trying to remember everyone's academic record from their earlier introduction. Most of them were much better qualified than me. I was firmly rooted in that bottom ten per cent as far as qualifications were concerned. Maybe I had bitten off more than I could chew. I knew very little about life as a policeman as I'd no relatives or friends in the job to offer advice. I didn't even know another copper. My limited knowledge about the police was picked up from what I had seen on TV. What if I didn't have the brains to pass those dreaded exams? Maybe I had good reason to feel apprehensive.

That first week at Wakefield passed by in a blur. An early morning session in the gym was usually followed by lectures in the classroom. I enjoyed the gym, could do that all day given the chance, but the classroom held less appeal. Then in the afternoon we'd spend an hour on the drill square. I was all arms and legs to begin with, but slowly began to make some progress. And in the evening the former cadets were suddenly in demand, demonstrating how to press our new uniform and bull our boots for the following day's inspection.

That first week, or the 'Induction Week' as it was called, prepared us for the next ten weeks at District Training School. We were destined for RAF Dishforth in North Yorkshire, a former airbase and now the regional police training centre for the northeast of England. No sooner had I got to know my West Yorkshire colleagues before we were split up again, now put in smaller groups of sixteen, probably because there just happened to be sixteen beds in each dormitory. For the day's classroom sessions we were joined by a couple of female colleagues, but in the evenings, and probably with good reason, the young ladies disappeared to their own bedrooms. For us blokes the accommodation was very basic; we each had a narrow metal-framed bed, and alongside it was a single wardrobe for all our earthly possessions. There was no TV or radio, no music, and worst of all, no comfort whatsoever. The accommodation had changed little since the end of the Second World War when it was used as an airbase. The place was still run on military lines, everyone in bed by eleven and then lights out.

Mornings started out on the drill square where the Camp Commandant would inspect our dress and deportment. Half an hour of drill practice and formation marching before a quick march into the classrooms for a day of tuition on criminal law. The training part of the day ended at 5pm and only then could we hang up the uncomfortable uniforms. Some form of sporting event took place on most evenings, maybe a session in the gym or football or badminton. At 9pm we could relax with a beer in the police bar, but not for long as by 10.30 the bar was closed. Then it was back to the dormitory and everyone tucked up in bed before the drill sergeant made his rounds.

It was an intense and high pressure existence, and for me there was a great deal at stake. I constantly worried about failing those exams, and possibly having to return to the building trade. Weekends at home provided little respite. I would arrive home late on Friday evening and spend the next 48 hours with my head buried in law books, revising for the exam which would take place the following Monday morning. The weekends passed far too quickly and by late

Sunday afternoon I was throwing my bags back into the car. The two hour drive back up the A1 motorway to Dishforth was a stressful trip, always worrying about the coming week and hoping to have enough time left for last minute revision before lights out.

Somehow I managed to pass all the exams, and most of them without too much difficulty, which perhaps showed that my earlier fears were unfounded. As one week merged into the next we were taught additional skills, such as how to carry out basic first aid; there were also many hours of self defence training, and we were taught the correct way to use a police truncheon and handcuffs. In the practical exercises we were instructed on how to operate the personal radios, always using the correct radio procedure, how to investigate a road traffic accident and arrest a shoplifter. There were life-saving qualifications in the swimming pool and riot training in an old aircraft hanger. We were taught how to take statements, carry out interviews and fill in endless forms and documents in preparation for life back at Division.

Finally, our initial training was over, ten weeks of hell were now behind us and we were told of our first postings. Brighouse was to be my destination, a small industrial town in West Yorkshire. That was great news, only a short drive from where I lived, a homely little place surrounded by the larger towns and cities of Bradford, Huddersfield and Halifax. I couldn't wait to leave training school and get stuck into some real policing.

CHAPTER 1

Daylight Robbery

I ambled along the canal towpath at a policeman's pace, a steady two miles an hour, hoping that I looked the part. It was midmorning in February. Today had started out just like yesterday, my third day of working the 'early turn' shift and another morning of pounding the beat.

Right now I didn't have a care in the world, alone with my thoughts and pondering on how my life had changed in recent months. That change had been so dramatic that sometimes I pinched myself when remembering that now I really was a copper. Five months ago it was a different story. Back then, in what seemed like a former life, I was struggling to make a living as a carpenter in the building trade. The sheer pace of that change sometimes took me by surprise, like this morning when I suddenly saw my own reflection in the window of the Co-op. I just happened to glance to my left and saw a uniformed copper staring straight back at me. Hard to believe, but that reflection was indeed me! Now, at least when I'm on duty, I have the title of PC 1021 Watson of the West Yorkshire Metropolitan Police, a hell of a shock to the system, but definitely a change for the better. I walked on, dragging myself away from those melancholic thoughts and back to the present. So this is it then, out on foot patrol, pounding the beat like generations of coppers before me.

I allowed myself a moment of self-satisfaction, feeling rather content with my lot. After all, I was outside in the fresh air. How many people, I asked myself, can earn their living by taking gentle exercise? Yeah, I thought, being a copper is not bad after all. I walked on, noticing the stark contrast between the murky water of the canal and the brightly painted narrowboats tied up alongside. How cozy those boats looked on this cold winter's day, the condensation running down the windows and smoke billowing from their metal chimneys.

Ahead, and to my left stood the nearest row of market stalls. Just about every type of trader was there, greengrocers, butchers and confectioners. Other stalls displayed children's clothing or hardware or kitchen utensils. There were traders selling books or pet food or handbags and suitcases. Pop music blasted out from the far side of the market with the latest hits, which probably annoyed the older generation. For the people of Brighouse this thriving little outdoor market catered for their every need. The raised voices of the stallholders rang out in the cold still air, each one competing with the constant pop music and all adding to the general hustle and bustle of the place.

It seemed to be just another perfectly normal day, but it would soon turn out to be anything but normal. I left the towpath and made my way through the market place, slowly wandering between busy stalls, smiling at the locals and saying my good mornings to faces that were starting to become familiar. The older stallholders had seen it all before, been here for generations and I was just the latest new copper to cut his teeth on their patch. Some couldn't resist sharing the odd comment or banter, they would joke about hiding the stolen goods until I had 'cleared off'. 'Who will give me £5 for this beautiful China Tea Set?' bawled one stall holder, women stopping to 'gawp' or carefully examine the goods. The same booming voice continued to ring out.

'No, I won't charge you £5 ladies, its not even £4, this beautiful crockery is available to you today for just £3, yes, you heard it right first time. I repeat, £3 ladies, now isn't that a real bargain?'

And so continued his familiar patter. One potential customer was already reaching for her purse, he pressed on with his polished performance, had them well and truly hooked and now he was reeling them in; but still he didn't let up.

'At this price I know what you lovely ladies are thinking, you think that this stuff must be stolen don't you? Well that's hardly surprising is it? I couldn't even buy them myself at this price.' He held centre stage in his carefully rehearsed piece of street theatre, and it wasn't the first time that he'd used this next line either.

'Oh bloody hell,' he suddenly yelled, whilst at the same time trying to appear shocked by my appearance. 'Here come the coppers,' he said, pointing an accusing finger in my direction, half a dozen heads simultaneously turning to face me. Without pausing for breath he continued with the bizarre sales pitch, shouting out to a youth on the other end of the stall, 'Quickly now Tony, come on lad, get a move on, get this stuff hidden under the stall till this bloody copper's gone.'

His performance was all part of a game, a game adopted by stallholders to get customers to part with their money. It was a routine that I was starting to become familiar with and the sort of thing I often heard when out on foot patrol. I was enjoying the friendly jovial atmosphere. I walked past the butcher's stall, listening to his sales pitch as he tried to compete with the banter of his neighbour. He held up joints of beef, or lamb, or fresh chickens. His booming voice promising shoppers the bargain of a lifetime. I gave him a friendly wave, acknowledged by him with no more than a discreet nod of the head. I ambled past, deciding that I'd been there long enough for now. 'See and be seen,' that was my sergeant's advice when walking the beat, but that would be for later in the day. Right now I intended to walk through town on my way back to the station, time to take the weight off my feet and sit down in the police canteen, enjoy a brew and a bacon sandwich for breakfast.

But things were about to change, up ahead, beyond the furthest market stalls, and towards the middle of the car park a crime was taking place. An elderly man emerged from a knot of people surrounding an old lady. They were carefully helping her back to her feet as this old chap waved at me. Walking with great difficulty, he could do little more than shuffle along. Something had obviously just happened that I had missed, and this old chap was going to tell me all about it. I hurried towards him and we met in the middle of the car park.

'It's Violet,' he told me, 'She's been mugged.'

Bloody hell, my heart suddenly raced to about 200 beats a minute.

'Is she alright?' I asked. 'Does she need an ambulance?'

He shook his head, barely able to speak, the poor old lad panted for breath and hung on to my arm for support.

'Just take it steady until you get your breath back,' I told him, I didn't want him keeling over after the sudden exertion. After a couple of deep breaths he was ready to tell me his tale.

Only now did the seriousness of this incident began to sink in. Come on Dave, I told myself, calm down and get a grip, work it through into some sort of logical sequence I told myself. Right, let's think straight, a street robbery has just taken place and that lady had been knocked to the ground. This old man saw a thief snatch her handbag before running away through this very car park. I looked across to where his shaking finger was pointing and saw that the victim was now back on her feet and being comforted by other shoppers. The poor old lass was unsteady on her pins, but luckily she appeared to be unhurt.

We were already starting to draw a crowd, people all around me stopped what they were doing to stand and listen. Suddenly I felt very self-conscious. Banter from the market stalls and the pop music had stopped. People stood and listened to this tale of woe, others anxious to see what was going on. Old and young alike gawped and they all expected me to know what to do next. A wave of apprehension swept over me, and I have to confess, I was more than a little nervous. I took another deep breath and tried to compose myself. This was indeed a street robbery, and that's a serious crime for a rookie-cop like me to deal with. In fact, I knew little about dealing with robbery and was out of my depth already. It was barely six weeks since I had left training school and there was still much to learn.

My brain wouldn't function properly, but I had to make important decisions, and make them quickly. During my first four weeks at Brighouse I was under the guidance of Steve, he was my tutor constable but that seemed like a lifetime ago. Steve wasn't the friendliest of blokes, but oh how I wish that he was here to help me now. A couple of weeks ago I had been deemed fit for independent foot patrol but I barely knew my way around the patch. Now I was expected to deal with a robbery with nothing like enough experience to deal with such a serious crime. A shoplifter would be easy enough, I'd already dealt with a couple of them, a drunken thug would be okay too. Even a minor car crash presented no real problems, but a robbery, well that was way beyond my ability, CID usually dealt with robberies, not rookie coppers like me. It was not the sort of thing I'd come across before and I was more than a little worried.

But today I would find out what the good people of Brighouse were really like. My head was spinning, what should I do first? I needed some advice before I really messed things up. So I did what every nervous copper would do; I radioed through to Control back at the nick, hoping that they would send someone out to help me, or failing that, at least tell me what to do. Regrettably, neither option was forthcoming, so I blindly looked round for inspiration, and soon discovered that these local folk would rise splendidly to the challenge. Some proved to be formidable amateur detectives, and together we did a far better job than I could possibly have managed alone.

As the seconds ticked by I tried to keep busy. First job was to record the details into my pocket book, just like I'd been taught at training school. As I was busy scribbling away a second witness approached, another elderly chap, at least seventy-five years old I reckoned, but still slightly younger than the first witness. He was positively wheezing and leaning heavily on his walking stick; the 20-yard dash had been a bit much for him. Not only did he see the robbery, he told me, but he had the presence of mind to watch the suspect run off into Bethel Street. Crucially, he saw that the thief was still holding the stolen handbag.

Armed with this new information, it was time to put away my pocket book and get moving. No point in writing down all those details when there was a possibility of making an arrest for robbery. 'Are you new round here lad?' asked the second witness.

'Yes,' I replied. 'Just started here.' He nodded his head slowly as he looked me up and down.

'Thought I hadn't seen you before,' he said, a knowing smile on his face. He then continued, 'Well lad, it looks like you're the new sheriff in town, and I guess that we'll be your deputies for today.'

So I gathered my deputies together and we all set off in a determined pursuit of the robber, the three of us moving at no more than a snail's pace towards Bethel Street. I ticked off the mental check list in my head, trying to arrange my thoughts in some sort of order: importantly, the victim was being looked after, I would get her details later; the witness to the robbery was with me, maybe he would be able to identify the suspect if we saw him; then there was the second old man, the chap who saw the suspect run into Bethel Street, he too was alongside me, but I noticed that the lenses in his glasses were so thick that he'd probably struggle to recognise his own wife, never mind the suspect; and of course there was me, and how useless had I been? I hadn't seen a bloody thing, even though I was only 30 yards away when the crime took place.

If only the robber knew, I thought to myself, that we were in hot pursuit, then surely he'd be quaking in his boots. With the long arm of the law closing-in he would probably surrender without a fight. But sadly it looked like I'd fallen at the very first hurdle. How on earth would I ever explain such a failure? I thought about the old lady, about the witnesses, and selfishly thought about what my sergeant would have to say about allowing a robber to escape. Barely two minutes had passed since we left the market but it looked like we'd lost him already. The damned thief had gone to ground, he'd made good his escape and disappeared off the face of the earth. No sign of him anywhere. Had he turned to the left or to the right or had ducked out of sight down one of the numerous back alleys? My heart sank and I was convinced that I'd let everyone down.

But just as I was about to give up the search and try to slink off with my tail between my legs, I had a welcome, and unexpected change of luck. By now, we were in Bethel Street when a third witness made himself known, and this time he wasn't quite as old as the first two, but then again he wasn't much younger either. This man would hold the key to detecting the crime. He had also seen our suspect, his attention being drawn to the fleeing thief after seeing him dispose of a ladies handbag in a litter bin. That sort of behaviour, he decided, was most unusual, so thankfully, this observant chap kept watch on the suspicious character and saw him enter a nearby cafe. The cafe was pointed out, not 50 yards from where we now stood. What a stroke of luck. So off we went again, marching, or maybe it was more like shuffling, along the footpath in the general direction of the cafe. Thankfully, this latest witness also wanted to join our gang, so the four of us strode purposely along Bethel Street. I looked round at my three trusty companions and made a quick estimate of their combined ages. It had to be more than 200 years, but they were looking to me, a raw recruit, for some sort of leadership. And what a frightening prospect that was!

Only a minute later I pushed open the door of the cafe, a clank from the ancient brass doorbell announcing our arrival. Nervously, I stepped inside followed by my newfound friends. It was my first visit to this cafe but a quick look round confirmed that there wasn't much to see. The large square room contained about a dozen tables. There was a counter over in the far right-hand corner and directly behind it was a small open plan kitchen. A balding man, tall and well-built, stood with his back to us as he leaned over the gas stove. He wore a blue and white striped apron and was busy with the frying pan preparing breakfasts, and was the owner of the café. He glanced over his left shoulder, a puzzled look on his face. And what a strange bunch we must have looked, three elderly gents and one fresh-faced copper straight from training school.

In the opposite corner was another internal door, bearing the nameplates of 'Toilet' and 'Emergency Exit', which gave me cause for concern, a possible escape route that would allow our man to sneak off again. A single fluorescent light hung from the ceiling and left the whole place feeling rather gloomy, made worse by condensation running down the windows. Nearly all the tables were occupied, ordinary folk out for morning shopping, having a chat with friends, maybe a cup of tea or a sandwich and a slice of home-made fruitcake.

Our entry had caused quite a stir, curious customers stopped eating or drinking and conversations ended as they turned to watch and listen. The four of us scanned the room looking for our suspect, then, one of my elderly witnesses stepped forward. He pointed out a man in the far corner who was sat by himself at a small table near that toilet door. I had obviously misjudged this old chap earlier. Despite those thick lenses in his specs, and his wheezy chest, he came up trumps when needed.

'That's him over there,' he confidently stated. 'He's the one you're after officer, that's the fella who ran off with t'old lasses handbag.'

'Aye,' agreed my third witness. 'It was him who I saw with t'handbag too.'

This was all sounding pretty conclusive, better than I could have possibly hoped for. What I really needed now was some physical evidence. I paused for a moment as the hushed voices behind me continued with their whispered conversations.

'Ooh I wonder what he's been up to? He looks a bit shifty he does.'

I was sure that everyone had stopped what they were doing, all intrigued by what was happening. Time for me to step forward, I walked towards the suspect, taking a good look at his face and noticed that he was trying to avoid eye contact. Guilt was written all over his ugly mug, a copy of the *Daily Express* held up in front of him in a futile attempt to hide behind it. Too late for that, this was the bloke we were looking for, the one who had dragged the old lady to the ground and run off with her handbag, and now identified by two of the witnesses.

Expectant eyes looked on from around the room, and for the first time I knew what it was like to have stage fright. Two more paces and I was at his table with my deputies right behind me. I paused and cleared my throat, had a quick look on the floor behind the suspect, no sign of a discarded handbag or purse. Nothing on his table or on any of the chairs; this bloke's no mug, he obviously dumped the evidence in the bin, just as my witness described. We stood in a circle around his table, looking down at him.

I leaned forward, resting the knuckles of both hands on his table, looking down at him and trying to appear threatening like some streetwise cop on TV, hoping to look like I really knew what I was doing, which of course I didn't. Then I spoke to him, a scruffy little man, aged about forty. I started by asking him if he'd been in the market earlier today.

'No, not me pal,' came back his confident reply. His shifty eyes returned to the newspaper in a vain attempt to ignore my presence, hoping that I'd just accept his half-hearted denial and move on to someone else.

It was so quiet that you could hear a pin drop, everyone straining their ears to see what would happen next. I was thinking exactly the same thing myself. The suspect's excuse, which I thought was offered far too readily, had obviously been rehearsed, and for me, self-doubt was starting to creep in. He had the appearance of being something of an old lag who knew all the answers, maybe he was hoping that a young copper like me would simply accept his story.

His confidence increased on sensing my self-doubt, but he was about to make a crucial mistake. His tongue was now working overtime, he said that he'd been in this cafe for at least ten minutes and hadn't set foot in the market all day. Probably thought that he was a convincing liar and confident that he could pull the wool over my eyes, but he hadn't taken into account that Ted, the cafe owner, was now also taking a keen interest in his story. The gas burner under the frying pan was quickly turned off as Ted leaned on the counter and listened intently to our conversation. He wasn't happy about what he'd just heard, and fortunately for me, he wasn't afraid of speaking out.

The words were barely out of the suspect's mouth before Ted's booming voice interrupted his explanation.

'Oh no you haven't,' he argued. 'You're a lying little bugger, you've only just walked in here, no more than two or three minutes ago, but you just hang on there for one minute . . .' He paused for a few seconds to collect his thoughts before saying to me: 'When this fella first came in . . .' There was another slight pause before Ted wagged his index finger up and down, finally pointing towards the toilet door. Then he spoke again: 'When he first came in here he went straight through there, to the toilet, and that was before he sat at that table. I thought it was a bit strange at the time.'

Looked like Ted didn't want to miss out on the action either. Perhaps he also wanted to be part of our gang, and right now I needed all the help I could get. Without a moment's hesitation Ted marched forward, past the suspect and pushed open the toilet door. Meanwhile, we all stood in silence and waited anxiously for the outcome. There was a rumble of dissent from other customers. They'd worked it out for themselves and had a pretty good idea of what had happened. It appeared that they weren't too happy about having a thief in their midst.

Within a minute Ted emerged from the toilet, now with a satisfied look on his face. He raised his right hand for all to see, he had the old lady's purse held in his meaty fist and now dripping with water. His booming voice announced to all present that he recovered the purse from inside the toilet cistern. He slapped the incriminating evidence down on the table directly in front of our suspect. The unhappy thief looked down at the table knowing that the game was up. Water seeped out of the sodden purse and formed a puddle on the table before dripping down onto his trouser leg. At last all the pieces were in place and I could make my first ever arrest for robbery.

Make this sound good Dave, I told myself, trying to steady my frayed nerves. 'Right, stand up,' I demanded, 'and put your hands behind your back, you're under arrest for robbery.'

The other customers now found their voices again, the general consensus being that I should forget all about arresting this evil man. Instead, he should be taken outside and hanged by his neck from the nearest lamp post. Such was their anger that I wondered if someone was, at that very minute, organizing a lynch party or scouring the streets for a strong rope.

The doorbell clanged again, and in walked the old lady who had been robbed. She walked slowly through the door. It had been a long walk for her, taken her almost five minutes to walk 200 yards. She was still a little shaky and was helped along by another lady of a similar age. Everyone turned to watch as she hobbled towards me. I told her to have a good look at the purse.

'Is this him?' she nervously asked, nodding at the hand-cuffed suspect.

Before I could answer Ted spoke out, 'Aye that's him love, I've found your purse but the money's gone, probably in this bugger's pockets. You sit yourself down love and I'll get you a cup of tea.'

She looked round for an empty seat but hesitated for a moment, then instead of sitting down she slowly approached the thief. She leaned heavily on her walking stick and, much to my surprise, she looked him in the eye and spoke directly to him. 'Why did you do it lad? I'm nearly eighty years old you know, and you could have hurt me bad, I'd give you the money if I thought you really needed it.'

If this thief hadn't felt guilty before then he certainly did now. He didn't have the courage to look her in the eye, but to his credit he did manage to mutter some sort of apology.

'I'm sorry love, really I am, don't know what came over me.'

One of my newly found deputies was already on his way out of the door to retrieve the handbag from the litter bin. The old lady sat down, she would be looked after in the cafe until a police car came to take her home. A statement would be taken from her later in the day and I called up for a car to transport my prisoner back to the nick. Within minutes my transport arrived and I left the cafe holding the thief by the handcuffs to shouts of, 'Well done lad,' and 'don't let the bugger out,' ringing in my ears.

Later that day I thought back to how the locals had helped me, little wonder that the hapless thief never stood a chance. Such incidents left me with a feeling of well-being, a real sense of job satisfaction, and maybe the belief that I really could make a small difference to the law abiding people of that town. Over the next couple of months my earlier reservations about whether I'd made the right career choice began to fade, and although I was not yet aware of it, I was to develop a deep affinity with the town and its residents. Brighouse was my first posting but I was already feeling that I would never want to leave the place.

CHAPTER 2

Beware of the Little Green Men

'Dave!' bellowed the inspector. 'You'll be going on prisoner escort duty in the van this afternoon.'

Damn, that was the last thing I wanted. Sorry Sir, but I'm going out to walk the beat in town, maybe call in at a couple of the shops for a chat and a brew, pass the time of day and catch up on the latest gossip. Well, that's what I hoped to do, but of course I didn't dare to tell him, instead I simply said, 'Yes Sir, no problem, who's going with me?'

'Hmn,' he mumbled, a pained expression now on his craggy face. 'Do you know Stanley Slater from down the valley at Todmorden?' Not a name I was familiar with I told him. 'Well, you'll know him after today. He's driving so you'll be in the back with the prisoners, and knowing what he's like it's probably the best place to be. Just make sure that you don't get abducted by aliens.'

And with that strange comment he turned on his heel and walked away. I didn't have the faintest idea what he was talking about and it looked like he didn't intend to enlighten me, but clearly my Inspector didn't have a very high opinion of Stanley.

At 2.30pm the police van pulled into the car park behind the nick. The driver stepped out, that must be Stanley I guessed. I watched him climb the half dozen steps towards the door, a small man, well, small for a copper anyway, slim build with thick dark hair. His most noticeable feature though was his deep-set, penetrating eyes, beneath thick, heavy brows, a sprightly but rather intense looking man. And

I was still puzzled by my inspector's comments about the aliens, no clues so far. Maybe I'd get the chance to quiz Stanley about it after dropping off the prisoners.

Soon we were loading the likely lads into the back of the van. Three teenagers climbed in first, all handcuffed together like prisoners in a chain gang. Sitting side by side on a long bench, they were all in high spirits, laughing and joking about their earlier appearance at court, their banter suggesting that they had never really expected to be released on bail in the first place. Still, at least it gave them chance to have a snatched chat with friends and relatives in the public gallery. A day out at court is better than another day cooped up in the Young Offenders' Institution (YOI). They sat down with elbows resting on knees, handcuffs restricting any arm movement. The unfortunate lad in the middle had drawn the short straw as he was shackled with a handcuff on each wrist. At least the other two had the luxury of having one hand free.

Opposite them sat Tommy, many years their senior and definitely something of an old lag. Earlier in the day he told me that he'd been out of prison for only six months. Foolishly, he was arrested this time after leaving fingerprints at a burglary, should know better at his age. Surely after twenty years of getting locked up he ought to know about wearing gloves. He was a sad case, made me think that maybe he wanted to get caught. Anyway, he would be back in Armley prison within the hour, back to his second home. For him the place was comfortable, three cooked meals a day and a bed for the night with the company of like-minded blokes. I climbed in the van and sat alongside him, the back doors were slammed shut, and moments later I heard Stanley snap the padlock closed. I was locked in the back of this tin box with four convicts, the only difference between us was that I would be going home tonight but my fellow passengers would be banged up in a prison cell.

Stanley climbed in the driver's seat and we moved off towards Leeds and Armley prison. Tommy would be the first one out, then it would be the long journey to Kirklevington to deliver the three young lads. There would be no contact with Stanley during this part of the journey. A solid bulkhead behind the driver's seat separates the front section of the van from the back, there to ensure that the driver remains safe. No such protection for me. Hopefully, today's prisoners were not likely to cause problems.

Forty minutes later we were pulling up at Armley. That first view of the prison entrance is certainly a daunting one. The two massive castellated turrets at the entrance gates are enough to frighten most people. Solidly built from Yorkshire gritstone, against the background of a grey sky, it's a visible sign of men's incarceration with the sort of history which legends are made. Hard to believe it now, but until about forty years earlier Armley was one of the prisons where the death penalty was still carried out, where murderers were hanged from the gallows by the official executioner. Our van stopped at the gates and I heard Stanley identify himself to the guards, he told them we had a prisoner from Brighouse magistrates' court. The gates swung open and Stanley drove slowly through into a central courtyard, now used as a car park. Moments later the back doors of the van were unlocked and I climbed out leading Tommy by the hand-cuffs. He knew which way to go and directed me through to the reception desk inside the prison buildings. It would be a frightening place to most people but Tommy now had a smile on his face and a spring in his step. Twenty minutes later the documentation was complete, Tommy was taken to a cell and I returned to our van to continue our journey north.

Again I sat in the back with the three remaining prisoners and we were soon speeding along the A1; and that was when my three fellow passengers started to mess around. Just a little horseplay really, or at least it was until the lad on the left leaned across his two mates and grabbed the handcuffs that they shared. He clasped their cuffs in his fist and scrunched his hands together. I heard the unmistakable sound of the ratchets tightening and clicking into place as he squeezed the two parts of the cuffs together. Seconds later, the steel cuffs were biting painfully into the wrists of his two mates. This lad knew what he was doing and the ratchet mechanism now locked in that much tighter position. It was a brief scuffle, over and done with in two or three seconds, and the perpetrator thought it was great fun. Understandably, his victims didn't share his sense of humour. Instead they howled and bounced around in agony, their hands first going numb before swelling up as the blood supply was cut off. The lad on the right wanted revenge, his turn to inflict a bit of pain himself, so he did exactly the same thing with the other pair of cuffs. Now all three of them shared the pain, and although it was amusing to sit and watch, I did feel rather sorry for the lad in the middle. With both wrists shackled, he bore twice the pain of the other two, and it was through no fault of his own.

I chuckled at their sense of fun, and of course their self-inflicted agony. Within minutes they were almost begging me for the handcuff key to loosen the cuffs but the key remained firmly in my pocket. In most circumstances unlocking a prisoner's cuffs would be far too risky for a solitary officer, but I figured that there was little to fear from these lads. They weren't exactly a threat to me, nor were they likely to escape from the van speeding along the motorway, so after delaying their release for a couple more minutes I complied with their wishes and loosened the cuffs.

It was late afternoon as we pulled up at Kirklevington YOI. It was very different in appearance to Armley prison. We were now in a rural setting rather than the inner city, and first impressions suggested that it was a much less intimidating place. Stanley remained in the van when I walked the first youth inside. He'd been here before and led the way as we went through an ordinary looking door opening out onto a long corridor. Directly opposite was the stable-type door used as a desk for the prisoner reception office. The top half of this door was wide open, a hatch, or improvised desk, rested on the lower half of the door. A big burly man dressed in prison officer's uniform stood up on our arrival and approached the desk, black trousers, white shirt, no tie, faded shoulder epaulettes showing a rank which meant little to me. Not the friendliest of greeting considering it my first time there, and as I was soon to find out, this man was something of a bully. 'Feet behind the line,' he barked at the lad stood alongside me. This young lad knew the rules, he looked straight down at the white tape stuck to the floor and quickly shuffled backwards until his toes were firmly behind it.

'Name?' continued the prison guard in the same brusque manner. The lad gave his name, surname first then Christian name. As it turned out he knew far more than I did, my first impression had been wrong, this place was equally as oppressive and threatening as the adult prison at Armley. Then, much to my surprise, another inmate came running along the corridor behind us. He ran straight past us and continued his charge along the corridor. He wore the usual inmates' garb and looked quite exhausted, struggling to keep his legs moving. I watched him run to the far end of the corridor where he touched the end wall with one hand before turning round and running straight back towards us. The lad was just about done in, sweating profusely and his face was glowing bright red, and for some unknown reason, he was carrying a full size fire extinguisher! No wonder he looked as though he was about to collapse. I guessed that the extinguisher must have weighed at least 20 or 30 pounds. I continued to watch as he staggered past us again. Less than two minutes later he was back, this time running in the opposite direction but still carrying the fire extinguisher, and by now he was nearly on his knees with exhaustion.

Within minutes the documentation was finished and my prisoner was led away. Only then did I speak to the brute who I took to be the senior officer. I asked him why that other lad was still running backwards and forwards along the corridor whilst carrying a fire extinguisher. His answer astounded me. The lad was being punished I was told. Apparently, he had been brought in from another court just before we arrived, and he failed to stand with both feet behind the line when addressing prison officers at this reception desk. Instead, he had the audacity to step forward and lean on the sacred desk. No wonder he was being punished so severely!

Armed with that information I returned to the van, ready to take the next lad through to the reception, still barely able to comprehend what I'd just heard. I warned the lad to keep his feet behind that white line, didn't want to see another youngster running up and down that corridor carrying a fire extinguisher. It was my first introduction to a young offenders' institution, and quite an eye opener it had been. Within the hour all three lads had been handed over and we could begin our return journey to Brighouse. Without the prisoners I could spend the rest of the journey sat in comfort in the front of the van, and it would give me the opportunity to delve into the mystery surrounding my driver.

We were back on the A1 before I dared to broach the subject of being abducted by aliens. But I'd never met Stanley before today, so should I start a conversation like that? He looked like a normal bloke to me, but the way my inspector spoke about him suggested that something wasn't quite right. I was looking for an opener – should I just come out with it and ask, 'Have you seen any aliens lately Stanley?' or even more bizarrely, 'I was just wondering, have you ever been abducted by aliens?' No, don't be stupid Dave, that would sound bloody ridiculous, this fella would think that I was bonkers, I'd have to be a little more subtle than that. Got it! Ask him about his life in Todmorden, always a good opener.

For several minutes there was an uncomfortable silence in the van. Time to take the plunge I reckoned. 'Now then Stan, how's life treating you down the valley at Tod?' I asked, trying to make the question sound like a casual enquiry.

Instantly, I knew that I'd hit a nerve, his head swivelled round to face me rather than watching the road ahead. He stared at me for a couple of seconds, maybe I'd just blown any chance of getting an answer. There was an awkward silence for several seconds and I guessed that he was trying to weigh me up. Now, was that really a genuine question? Or was this young copper taking the mickey? His next question suggested that he was prepared to give me the benefit of the doubt.

'You haven't heard then?' he asked.

'Heard what?' I replied innocently.

'Haven't you heard that I don't work at Tod anymore? The bosses got windy about the newspaper headlines, so they've moved me. I usually work at the cells at Halifax nick now.'

What a relief. Despite my opening question it seemed like he was willing to talk about it after all.

'No, I didn't know,' I answered. 'They just told me that you would be coming to pick me up, said that you'd be driving the prisoner van, and I was going along as your escort.'

By pure chance it seemed that I'd given him the opening that he was looking for. Maybe it was a chance to tell his story to someone who was not already prejudiced by rumours. And once he started talking the floodgates opened. Without a break in the conversation he continued his tale all the way back to Brighouse, and what an incredible story it turned out to be.

It started in November 1980, almost a year before I joined the police, which is why it was all new to me. He had been working a night shift in his home at Todmorden, a small town high up in the Pennine hills. As usual he was on mobile patrol driving a panda car and his last job of the night was to round up a herd of cows wandering about in the road. It was after five in the morning and he'd be off duty in less than an hour, but he found no trace of the cows. Dismissing the job as a false call, he gave up the search and started making his way back to the police station. But then he saw something unusual up ahead, he initially thought was a bus slewed across the road with its lights blazing. Only on getting closer did he realise that it wasn't a bus after all. The intense light was actually coming from a cylindrical object which Stan believed was a UFO. It hovered some five feet above the ground with windows in the top half whilst the bottom half rotated in an anti-clockwise direction.

Wow, I thought, this is going to be some story, but was this bloke winding me up, or did he really expect me to believe that he had seen a spaceship on the hills above Todmorden, a place not 20 miles from where I work? I didn't know what to believe, but his tale was passing the time quite nicely, and

I have to say that he was a convincing storyteller, so I urged him to continue.

'Then what happened?' I asked, wondering where this strange tale was heading.

'Well at the time I didn't really know,' he replied. 'But somehow I ended up back in the police car and I was still driving along the same road. But I knew that no one would believe me about a UFO, not unless I could find another witness.'

'Yeah, I suppose that's true, so did you find anyone?'

Stan continued with his tale, telling me that he then drove into Todmorden town centre where he met another officer on foot patrol. He told his colleague what had happened and somehow persuaded the trusting fellow to accompany him back to where he last saw the UFO. They left the town centre behind and were soon heading out of the valley. After a couple of miles Stan pointed out the mysterious location and pulled over on to the grass verge and parked up. They climbed out of the car to make a closer examination. Despite the recent rain, Stan pointed out that the ground there was somewhat drier than the surrounding area. This was exactly the same spot where he saw the UFO hovering. Now they found yet another strange phenomenon, there was a circle of leaves and twigs lying on the ground, torn from surrounding trees and shrubs. He believed that this was as a result of the rotation effect created by the UFO.

Evidence indeed one may think! However, fearing that if it became public knowledge he would be ridiculed, Stan persuaded his colleague that it would be best to keep quiet about the incident. But on arriving back at the station Stan checked the time and realised that he couldn't account for a lost period of about fifteen minutes in the last hour. This missing fifteen minutes was a complete mystery to him and that morning he left the police station with many unanswered questions.

Later that day further evidence came to light which appeared to back up Stan's own experience. It turned out that at about the same time as Stan's unexplained incident another local man had driven along the same road. Although this man was three miles further out of Todmorden than Stan had been, he too saw a strange phenomenon. Interestingly, this new witness described seeing a brilliant white object in the sky. And he was so concerned about the incident that he later went to Todmorden police station to make a formal report. So on returning to work later Stan heard that there was now corroborating evidence and decided to report his own experience. Over the coming days and weeks all the hype and publicity snowballed which would later threaten to overwhelm him. Within weeks his story was headline news in the Sunday papers, much of it causing the sort of publicity not always appreciated by some senior officers within the police force.

Stan told me that when this story became public he fully expected to be mocked by colleagues. But what he didn't expect was that some senior officers would openly question his sanity, and even try to hound him out of the Force. His enforced transfer from his home town of Todmorden was one such example. However, help was at hand, and it came from a very unexpected source. A group of UFO enthusiasts from Manchester contacted him and offered their assistance. Stan explained that this group included some very eminent people, doctors, barristers and the like. Crucially, they appeared to believe his story, and were prepared to help him prove it to be true.

In the coming months Stan sought their advice, even allowing himself to be hypnotically regressed by a psychiatrist. Obviously it was hoped that he would recall the incident in greater detail whilst under hypnosis. And this was when I really started to doubt his story.

He told me that when under hypnosis he had recalled seeing a brilliant white light which somehow caused the car engine to stop. This light also rendered both the car radio and his personal radio inoperative. Then he lost consciousness. Sometime later he woke but was no longer in the police car. Although Stan could offer no explanation he now found himself inside some sort of room. Maybe he was even inside the UFO. Also in that room was a man called 'Yosef'. With him were several assistants, all having the appearance of small robots. And perhaps the strangest thing of all was the presence of a large black dog. Josef had a long beard, he wore flowing robes and was biblical in appearance, and communicated with Stan by way of telepathy.

Blimey, was this bloke really suggesting that he'd had direct connection to the big fella upstairs? Or if not the top man himself then he must at least have met one of the Apostles. This was all too much for my doubting mind. He gave me a sideways look, sensing that I doubted his story and that's where he cleverly decided to play his trump card.

'I get the impression that you don't believe me, do you Dave?' he asked, maybe it was more of a statement rather than a question.

'Well, you have to admit that it's a bit unusual, and coppers are sceptical people by nature aren't they,' I replied. 'You know what its like, we always want to see the evidence or the proof of something don't we? Something tangible that we can see or feel or touch.'

I'm sure he was expecting my reaction, probably seen it many times before and his answer was already prepared. He asked if I knew of three particular police officers who he named, all working at Halifax. Two of them I knew only by reputation, the third one I had never heard of. However, the two who were known to me were both well regarded officers, known for being level-headed and hard-working blokes. Stan then played his ace.

'So I suppose that you'd be surprised to hear that those three were working nights, up on the moors above Halifax, and they saw the same thing as me. Well maybe not the whole thing but they did see an unexplained blue, or possibly a white light descending towards Todmorden, and it was at the same time that I saw the UFO.'

I was gobsmacked, now I really didn't know what to think. This story fell into two parts as far as I could see. The first part was that Stan claimed to have seen a UFO. Well that's not too unusual, I reminded myself that the letter 'U' simply stands for 'Unexplained' and that's exactly what it appeared to be. Stan's account was, at least in part, corroborated by at least one member of the public and maybe by other police officers who had no reason to verify his story if it wasn't true. But if I was to believe Stan about seeing a UFO then what about the second part of his story? The bit about him being abducted by aliens, or fifteen minutes of his life left unaccounted for. Had he really spent that time inside that spacecraft as he was suggesting?

He was certainly a good storyteller, but was he just a convincing fantasist or had he really experienced something which was quite beyond my comprehension? I came to the conclusion that I would never know the answer. There was only one man who knew the truth, and that was Stan himself. I had to accept that if he was telling me the truth then at least I'd heard it straight from the horse's mouth and not from rumours within the police or from the Sunday tabloids. The whole thing left me not knowing what to think, but I certainly wouldn't be quite as dismissive as my inspector had been earlier. By the time Stan finished recalling the events of that fateful night we were nearly back at Brighouse where he dropped me off before returning to Halifax. For the last two hours I had listened to his remarkable tale, and if nothing else it had been a fascinating account.

However, there was one thing of which I was quite certain, whether Stan was relating fact or fantasy didn't really matter. What did matter though, and something that I was sure about, was that HE believed it to be true. I climbed out of the van convinced that Stan believed every word of it.

At the start of the day I expected nothing but routine police work, almost to the point of tedious boredom. But the day turned out to be anything but boring. Later, as I drove home from work, I reflected on the day, smiled at the joviality show by the three lads who were now locked up at Kirklevington. I felt a certain amount of sympathy for Tommy living the life of a relatively inoffensive but habitual burglar who saw prison as an occupational hazard. And then there was Stan, I'd never met anyone quite like him, with a tale so extraordinary that I will probably remember it till the end of my days.

A few years later I heard that Stan had left the police after an injury on duty. By that time I guess that some senior officers were glad to see the back of him, and he probably felt exactly the same about them. He had, I'm sure, been hounded out of the police after all the publicity surrounding his extraterrestrial experience.

CHAPTER 3

Merry Christmas

It was Christmas Eve 1982, my first Christmas of walking the beat in Brighouse town centre. So much had happened in the last twelve months, yet it felt like only yesterday that I was still a raw recruit. Back then I had just finished at police training school and was allowed a day off work to spend Christmas Day at home.

'Make the most of it,' said my new sergeant, 'it's not likely to happen again for a good few years.'

Sadly his prediction proved to be right and this time I was working the dreaded night shift. Just before ten I sat down for the team briefing and found myself envying my mates with normal jobs. They would be out on the town celebrating rather than pounding the streets of Brighouse. Sergeant Dykes came into the room and stood at the lectern to start the briefing, telling everyone their duties for the next eight hours. Slowly it dawned on me that everyone else apart from me would be either double crewed in the panda cars, or they'd be in the Transit van on public order patrol. Then he glanced briefly in my direction before coming up with the inevitable.

'Dave, you're out on foot patrol in town, come in for your meal at two o'clock, then you're back in town again after your meal.' Oh great, I thought, my colleagues would be all inside a comfortable, warm car or van but I'll be out in the cold pounding the beat by myself.

So that was it, briefing over. As the junior member, or the 'rookie' on our team, I'd be pounding the beat. I had hoped that maybe in this season of good will to all men that

Sergeant Dykes would soften a little and allow me to ride around in the back of the van. No chance Dave, this bloke didn't have a sympathetic bone in his body.

With the briefing over Sergeant Dykes gathered up his papers and left the room, time for my colleagues to start winding me up. 'Oh don't worry Dave,' joked Ray. 'At midnight the drunken birds will come pouring out of the pubs wanting a big sloppy kiss, it's like that every Christmas.'

Should I look forward to such an outpouring of good cheer, or try to avoid it? I was unsure, but I'd find out soon enough. Ten minutes later I left the nick and began my solitary walk along Bradford Road into town, bundled up against the cold night with the heavy police greatcoat covering the rest of my uniform. The temperature had dropped a few degrees in the last hour but at least it was dry, and there was little wind, so it could have been much worse. I consoled myself with that thought; and surely this should be a night for enjoyment rather than one for trouble.

On entering the town centre, I checked my watch, nearly 10.30 already. For some reason the streets were unusually quiet, especially for Christmas Eve. I couldn't help but wonder where the revellers were all hiding. Back at the nick my colleagues gave the impression that the streets would be packed.

I walked slowly on, passed the raised flowerbed in Thornton Square, displaying its huge Christmas tree draped with coloured lights. After the first circuit of town I paused for thought. My earlier assessment had been slightly wrong, the streets weren't completely deserted after all. There was the odd drunk staggering about, men who had probably been out on the beer all day, a few courting couples dashing from pub to pub with arms wrapped tightly around each other to fend off the cold. Then up ahead a large group of young people made for the George Hotel. Could be the overspill from an office or works party I guessed, all rather loud and boisterous but in good spirits and obviously enjoying themselves. I had only a fleeting glimpse of them and found it difficult to tell what gender they were. Most of the group were wearing fancy dress costumes belonging to the opposite sex. They all disappeared into the pub. The lucky devils will probably stay there boozing away until midnight.

I continued my sedate foot patrol around town, met few people but noticed how friendly they seemed to be compared to other times of the year. Young men walking past would purposely reach out to shake my hand, usually followed by a jovial 'Merry Christmas officer'. Young women, and sometimes women who were not quite so young, would make sure that their dentures were firmly in place before demanding a Christmas kiss. Many of them would ask their friend to take a photograph and record the event, usually when they were linking arms with me and wearing my police helmet. There I stood, slightly embarrassed and staring into the camera with a silly grin on my face.

From Commercial Street I turned left into Park Street and then right into Bethel Street, just in time to see a group of about a dozen young men disappearing into the Prince of Wales pub. I didn't recognize any of them, which struck me as being unusual. It also triggered an alarm bell. For almost twelve months I'd walked this foot beat almost every day. By now I knew the regular drinkers in town, and that particular group were not regulars. Looked more like outsiders to me, which is not a good sign.

I knew that some of our regular drinkers took a dislike to outsiders, it was an attitude which could spell trouble later on in the night. I made a mental note to keep my eyes open for that group. Still, it should be easy enough to spot them again as they all wore identical clothing, distinctive green and black rugby shirts and jeans. Probably from one of the amateur rugby clubs in a neighbouring town. Although, on second thoughts, they did look like a pretty tough bunch of blokes. At least I wouldn't have to worry too much about the locals picking a fight with them which usually happens when outsiders come drinking in this town.

As the next hour slowly passed I realised that although the streets appeared to be fairly quiet, the pubs themselves were absolutely packed with drinkers. A glimpse through any open pub door or window would reveal a mass of people inside. After midnight all these people were going to hit the streets at exactly the same time. And by then, many of them would be struggling to stand up.

Self doubt was starting to creep in. How would I cope if there was trouble? Worryingly, I hadn't seen another copper, or even a passing police car in the last hour. And where were the coppers in the police van who were supposed to be on public order patrol? On any other weekend the van would be highly visible, patrolling the town centre, they would often park up outside the pubs, but obviously not tonight. It would be reassuring for me to know that help was at hand if things did turn nasty, especially when all the drunks spilled out on to the streets.

There was another reason for me to feel concerned, I'd noticed that the radio messages were becoming progressively busier and busier, and the panda cars and van crew were being diverted away from town to jobs out in the suburbs. I was on my own and starting to feel just a little bit vulnerable, slightly nervous now and somewhat apprehensive. I silently cursed Sergeant Dykes for sending me out like this, on what was likely to be the busiest night of the year.

I took a couple of deep breaths and tried to put such fears behind me, after all I was probably worrying about something and nothing. One more circuit around the town then another quick check of my watch, it was 11.55, Christmas Day only five minutes away, and I was almost counting down the minutes. Now, the streets really were deserted, all those lucky people packed inside the pubs waiting for the clock to strike midnight. Yeah, it's all right for some people, inside a lovely warm pub with all their mates and a beer to celebrate the start of Christmas. And here I am, billy-no-mates, stood outside the Round Tavern Pub all by myself, chilled to the bone and stone cold sober. I could think of better ways to spend Christmas Eve.

But maybe I'm not going to be alone, there's a strange looking woman running towards me. She's waving frantically to attract my attention. It must be difficult to run in that short red mini-skirt, and she's wearing fishnet tights covering her skinny legs. What a strange sight she is with her slim waist and narrow hips, completely out of proportion to her broad shoulders. I didn't really know what to make of her, then, as she came closer I noticed her thick eyebrows and heavy jaw, her large nose and deep-set eyes. But she's not really running, hobbling would be a better description, and she's definitely coming my way, waving her hand above her head and shouting something which I can't quite make out. I notice that she's limping. Oh yes, I've just seen the reason why, she's wearing only one of her high-heeled shoes, and carrying the other in her left hand. Several yards behind her is another woman. She's much shorter in height and very rotund, and for some reason she seems to be having great difficulty in walking. The second woman appears to be so drunk that she's now stopped walking altogether and is leaning against the shop windows. I hope that she's not throwing up everywhere.

I look back to the first woman, what a fearful sight she is, tall and lanky, and to put it mildly, unattractive. I just hope that she doesn't try to kiss me! But there's a touch of panic in her voice which sounds rather deep and coarse.

'Please help us,' she croaked, 'it's my wife,' she pointed back along the street towards the other woman. 'Her waters have broken and she's gone into labour.'

Now I thought that I'd heard her right but surely I'd misheard that last sentence? 'What, what did you just say, what on earth are you talking about?' I asked. Now it was my turn to panic.

'The baby's coming, you need to get an ambulance here quick.'

Bloody hell, a baby. Oh no, I didn't need telling twice. I squeezed the transmit button on my radio and shouted to Frank in the radio control room.

'1021 to Control, get me an ambulance to King Street, there's a woman here who's about to give birth, and please, tell them that it's really urgent.'

Frank, our seasoned radio operator, was calmness personified, a man who'd seen it all before and was totally unruffled, the exact opposite to what I was feeling. It was only a few seconds earlier that I suddenly realised that the 'ugly woman' was really a man, dressed in drag, and the 'rotund' female staggering behind him happened to be his heavily pregnant wife. This unfortunate female was now leaning against the window of the Co-op in King Street.

With a racing heart I dashed towards her, but still didn't have a clue what I was supposed to do. The poor woman was in real distress, arms spread on the window and legs similarly spread on the pavement as though she was being frisked in an American cop movie. Her breathing was coming deeply and quickly and her face was screwed up with pain. I glanced across at her husband, saw that he had removed his other high-heeled shoe and now held them both in one hand. He reached up to run his free hand through his hair and suddenly remembered the long silver wig. The wig was quickly dragged off his head and held in the same hand as the shoes.

'Can't you do something?' he pleaded. But before I could offer any words of comfort he turned his attention back to his wife. 'Susan, Susan, listen to me, it's all right sweetheart, this policeman will help you, he's just called for an ambulance so you've got to hang on.'

'But it's coming Tony, the baby's coming. Tony I'm frightened,' she screamed.

It wasn't only this young woman who was frightened, her husband was in a similar state, and I too wasn't far behind them.

I had studied basic First Aid at training school last year, even had to pass a written exam, but for the life of me I couldn't remember doing anything about childbirth. What the hell was I supposed to do, stuck here on a town centre street at midnight? It was Christmas Eve and I didn't have so much as a sticking plaster or a paracetamol at my disposal, and this woman was about to give birth. No wonder I was so bloody frightened.

But sadly I was the only uniformed presence, the one person who the public turned to in an emergency, and as far as I was concerned, this was certainly an emergency. I had to do something, her husband was right, it was my duty to do something, but what? So, unable to think of anything useful, I resorted to shouting back into my radio again.

'1021 to Control, this woman is about to give birth, I need some help here urgently.'

Oh how my colleagues would be laughing at my predicament, they'd hear the panic in my voice, glad it was me and not them who was lumbered with this job. And of course now that they'd heard all about it, they were sure to keep well away. I don't know what sort of reply I expected, but when it came it didn't help.

'Control to 1021, please calm down, there's no need to panic. The ambulance is on its way and will be with you anytime now.'

Our laid-back radio controller was right about one thing, I was definitely panicking, my heart hammered against my chest and sweat ran down my back despite the freezing temperature.

'But there must be SOMETHING you can do,' pleaded her husband. He gently rubbed his wife's back as she shivered and moaned in the cold night air. I could think of only one thing to help, keep her warm, yes that's what I could do. I was wearing full uniform including a sweater, a tunic and this thick woollen greatcoat, hardly surprising that I was now sweating. And that's what people always seem to do when someone is injured in a car crash don't they? So I took off my coat and draped it around her shoulders, no point in trying to fasten the buttons, the bulge of her stomach was far too large for that.

'Why don't you sit down here love,' I suggested. 'Just sit down and pull my coat around your shoulders?'

A moment later and she was doing just that, there, at last I'd done something useful. I had to admit that it wasn't much, but at least it was something. Unbeknown to her, there was method in my madness, she was now sat firmly down on the one part of her anatomy which was about to become the source of further turmoil. I reasoned that if she remained sat on that hard surface, then the very problem which I was most dreading was less likely to make an early appearance.

She had gently lowered herself down on to the cold pavement and leaned her shoulders back against the shop window, trying to shuffle into a comfortable position on the ground. Her knees were bent up and tucked into her chest, her legs wide apart, and her short maternity dress barely covered her assets. Tony tried his best to reassure his wife, kneeling down on the pavement and staring at the very place from where his child was about to emerge, probably at any second now. For my part I was trying to look anywhere but there, the whole process terrified me. The last thing I wanted to see was a baby's head emerging from between this poor woman's legs.

Suddenly I heard the sound of fireworks in the distance. I looked towards the hills to the east of the town and saw the bright colours light up the sky above the village of Clifton. What a sight it was, dozens of rockets streaming up into the dark sky on the stroke of midnight, the start of Christmas Day. From 30 yards behind me the clientele from the Round Tavern pub were celebrating by pouring out of the pub and onto the street. The sound of Noddy Holder and Slade blasted out from the juke box: *So here it is Merry Christmas, everybody's having fun.* Well, you may be having fun Noddy, but I certainly wasn't. Crowds of people were singing and celebrating only yards behind me, totally unaware of the drama taking place on our side of the street. Then I heard another woman's voice shouting out.

'Susan, hey Susan is that you, hello love, it's Caz, are you all right love?' A moment later Caz appeared behind me, she was one of the crowd that had just left the Round Tavern and was obviously a friend of Susan. Tony moved away for a moment and Caz took his place. She knelt down in front of Susan, gently stroking her friend's face to comfort her.

'Oh Caz please help me,' pleaded Susan. 'I wasn't due for another week but my waters have broken and it's coming now, the baby's coming.'

I was praying that Caz would know what to do. Surely all females know more about childbirth than an ignorant bloke like me. A small crowd started to gather round, some just watching, others asking what was going on. Susan suddenly screamed out in agony, a high-pitched, terrifying wail. Caz responded, now with a real sense of urgently in her voice.

'We'll have to take her knickers off, I think the baby is coming,' her shrieking voice informing everyone within ear-shot. She looked up at me and Tony. 'You two will have to help, I can't do it all by myself, you lift her up and I'll take her knickers off.' We were in no position to argue. Now my heart was really racing as we gently lifted an arm apiece. Susan's bum was lifted off the pavement and Caz whipped off the knickers. They were quickly discarded on the pavement. I watched Caz with admiration, she was really excelling in her new role as a midwife. Then I heard the words I was dreading, when she leaned forward and peered between Susan's outstretched legs.

'I think I can see the head, the baby's coming, move back everyone so she can lay down.'

Oh no, I really did not want to see a baby's head, not tonight of all nights, but at least Caz seemed to be taking charge. The crowd shuffled back, created a little space and suddenly all sorts of questions were flying through my fuddled head. Should we try to move Susan off this cold pavement and get her inside the pub? What about the umbilical cord? What if there were complications and the cord was wrapped around the baby's neck? Too many questions but no answers.

Caz, however, was doing a splendid job, if nothing else she was taking some of the pressure off me.

'It's alright Susan, you just keep breathing deeply, yes that's it. The contractions are coming quicker now but you must try to breath slowly, in ... out ... in ... out ... yes that's good but you mustn't push yet Susan.'

I glanced across at Tony, we each held one of Susan's hands as Caz concentrated on what was happening at the business end. I sneaked another look at him and noticed that he was following the instructions that Caz gave to Susan. I watched in fascination and saw that he too was taking deep slow breaths, just as Caz had demonstrated. Then to my horror I realised that I too was doing exactly the same. I was instantly brought back to reality by the voice of a young girl coming from behind me.

'Hey you, Mr Policeman, what's your name?'

I turned round to look at her, a pretty little thing dressed as a fairy, presumably the fairy from the top of a Christmas tree, complete with a pair of silver wings strapped to her back.

'It's PC Watson,' I answered. 'Why do you want to know?'

'No, I don't mean your last name, what's your first name?'

'It's David, why?'

'Well David, if it's a baby boy, and you deliver it, Susan will want to name him after you,' she said. 'That's what happens on telly anyway.'

The thought that these people expected me to deliver a real live baby, here in the street, almost frightened me to death. Up to this point in my life I had managed to avoid ever holding a baby, and now I was expected to deliver one!

Behind me a long snake of Christmas revellers danced out of the pub doing the conga. Most of them were drunk and singing their heads off until suddenly the whole line came to an abrupt stop. The man leading the chain saw us and put on the brakes.

'Oye, what's going on over there?' he bellowed.

The Christmas tree fairy answered. 'It's Susan!' she shouted back. 'She's having her baby, it's coming now and this policeman is going to deliver it, and if it's a baby boy she's going to call it David, after him, don't you think that's sweet?'

Oh no, no, no, please shut up, please don't make things any worse than they already are. We now had an audience of nearly fifty drunken people, all watching my every move. I just wanted the ground to open up and swallow me. But at that very moment I heard the welcome sound of ambulance sirens in the distance, thank goodness for that, my saviours were coming, suddenly there was hope that I might get through this thing.

'Just you hang on Susan,' I told her, 'I can hear the ambulance, it will be here in a minute.' She was now certainly taking deep breaths and I felt her fingernails digging into the back of my hand.

One minute slowly passed, then another, the audience were getting inpatient, Susan was becoming desperate and I'm sure that Tony and I were both on the verge of nervous breakdowns. Every second felt like an hour, surely that ambulance should be here by now but where the hell had it gone? An awful thought occurred to me, perhaps those sirens didn't belong to an ambulance after all, maybe it was a police car or even a fire engine. Panic was starting to grip me again. Susan had stopped the heavy breathing, instead it was now continuous screaming and wailing, which was even worse. Caz was still valiantly knelt down between her friend's legs and provided little comfort when she said, 'It's coming Susan, I don't think it will wait any longer. You're going to have to push when you feel the next contraction.'

Now I am not a religious man but I have to confess that at that very moment I was saying a silent prayer to ask our Lord for deliverance from this living hell. Then, in the distance, the best sight in the whole world appeared. Two flashing blue lights on the roof of an ambulance, and thankfully it was heading our way. Never have I been so glad to see an ambulance arrive. The delay was caused by the driver conforming to the one-way system by driving all the way around the perimeter of town rather than take the shorter, and more direct route through the no entry signs, but that didn't matter now.

The ambulance stopped alongside us, two medic men were out of their vehicle in seconds and Susan was lifted from the pavement and quickly strapped onto a trolley to be wheeled into the back. Then, before the doors were slammed shut the driver leaned out and asked if anyone other than Tony wanted to accompany Susan to the maternity ward. Caz didn't want to miss out.

'Wait for me, I'll come with you.' She headed for the ambulance doors and was about to climb aboard when she stopped and looked back at me, and with a cheeky smile said, 'Are you coming too officer? You never know it might be a boy.'

Nice try love, I thought to myself, but you've got no bloody chance, no chance whatsoever, but I'd better try to appear professional. 'Sorry Caz but I can't, I have to stay on foot patrol in the town centre.'

The ambulance was soon on its way, with blue lights flashing. The conga dancers regrouped and continued their dance around the town but I needed a cup of hot sweet tea. I picked up my coat intending to head for the taxi office, my usual tea spot when working nights. Then as I moved off I glanced down at the pink knickers lying on the pavement. No, I wouldn't be taking them back to the nick as lost property, they could stay there as far as I was concerned. I walked away thinking about what could have happened if the ambulance had been delayed by just another five minutes. It was a close escape for me, far too close for comfort.

It wasn't yet one o'clock in the morning. I hadn't even been on duty for three hours but already I was feeling physically drained. I put on my coat and headed towards Huddersfield Road and the taxi office, hoping that I'd get a few minutes reprieve; and a chance to sit down in comfort with a cup of tea and hopefully a bit of peace and quiet.

Within minutes I was in the taxi office and sufficiently recovered to include a touch of frivolity when telling the tale of my brush with childbirth. The waiting taxi drivers chuckled at my tale of woe. It no longer seemed quite so frightening now that I was sat in the safety of their office sipping a cup of freshly brewed tea. George, the owner of the business, had provided a selection of sandwiches and cakes for his employees. I was just about to tuck into a mince pie when I was suddenly interrupted. It was Bill, one of the regular drivers. He burst into the office looking flustered, with a concerned expression etched onto his face. He looked straight at me and then, with his thumb, he gestured back towards the door.

'You'd better get yourself out here Dave, looks like all hell's breaking loose.'

I grudgingly put down the tea and half-eaten mince pie to follow Bill outside. He stood in the doorway and pointed towards the roundabout not 50 yards away. No longer looking like a roundabout, now it resembled a battlefield.

The centre of the roundabout was usually surfaced with traditional cobblestones but in recent days the stones had been lifted to access a leaking underground drain. Workmen carrying out the repair had simply piled the stone cobbles in the edge of the road so that they could be re-laid when the drainage work was complete.

Those cobbles were now being used as ammunition. I watched in horror as a young thug hoisted one of these stones high into the air towards an oncoming mob. His actions reminding me of a shot-putter in an athletics event. One of his mates employed a different technique, he bowled the stones underarm like a competitor in a game of ten pin bowling. The stones bounced along the road surface, turning end over end before crashing into the legs of the attackers. Bill followed me out and stood alongside me.

'Drunken idiots, it's like Custer's last stand at the Alamo,' he said, laughing at his own description of the scene. He was clearly enjoying the spectacle, but my job was supposed to prevent incidents like this. He knew that I was worried and I think he felt some sympathy on seeing my dilemma. He rubbed his chin, searching for a few words of comfort.

'Ah, don't you worry about it Dave, there's nowt you can do about it lad, leave the silly buggers to it. If they want to kill each other, let 'em get on with it.'

The thugs who were hurling the stones all wore rugby shirts, it was the same men I'd seen earlier. I watched in trepidation as they expertly launched their ammunition at a mob of local drunks charging along the road to attack them. Some sort of disturbance had obviously taken place when I was in the taxi office. It was now reaching a climax in a pitched battle right in front of me. I stepped down the two steps from the office doorway and walked towards the melee but what could I do by myself? Bill was right, I needed back-up, there was no way that I could deal with an incident like this without help.

'1021 to Control,' I shouted down the radio. 'I need some back-up in Bradford Road urgently, there's about thirty blokes in a mass brawl and they're hurling cobblestones at each other, I need some help before someone gets killed.'

The radio operator was getting fed up with me tonight, in the last hour I'd called in two jobs. According to my descriptions they were both emergencies where I needed urgent back-up, and they came at a time when everyone else was already busy at other incidents. His reply didn't fill me with confidence.

'1021, yes we've received your message, it's logged on the computer. Can you just monitor the situation and keep us informed, we'll get you some help when someone comes free.'

When someone comes free! What the hell is that supposed to mean? I needed help now, not in five or ten minutes. The two opposing groups had now come together, fists and feet lashing out in every direction. I stood in the newsagent's shop doorway and watched, not 20 yards from the melee. The opposing gangs were oblivious to my presence, or maybe they simply didn't care that one solitary, uniformed copper was stood watching a mini riot take place. They simply ignored me and carried on beating seven bells out of each other. I was no more than a spectator, a fly on the wall on the edge of this mass brawl of flying fists and flailing feet, shouts and screams and threats and abuse. Young men were being punched or kicked to the ground where they either curled up in a ball, or tried to get back to their feet to join in the brawl again.

It went on for only a couple of minutes, although it seemed much longer than that before I heard the welcome sound of sirens approaching. There was a momentary lull in the fighting when the combatants looked up and saw a police Transit van speeding towards them, and then, as if by magic the fighting suddenly stopped.

The rugby-shirted warriors gathered themselves together, picked up one or two of their fallen comrades, and jogged away. They ran towards the taxi office just as a mini-bus was returning to base to collect the next fare. It was a relief when they all crammed into the mini-bus and were quickly whisked away and out of town.

The opposing youths also quickly drifted away, leaving in small groups of twos and threes, all seeming to melt away into the night, none of them prepared to hang around and run the risk of being arrested. Half a minute later the van screeched to a halt and my colleagues stepped from it to find the street just about deserted. The only evidence that a battle had taken place were dozens of cobblestones now littering the roadway.

The sergeant remained sat in the van as I gave him a detailed account of what happened, but somehow I had the impression that he didn't quite believe me.

'Right Dave,' he said, 'Well it's all quiet now so we'll leave it with you.' And with that he ordered his troops back into the van. They were just about to leave when he wound down the window again and left me with his parting shot.

'Oh, and one more thing Dave, do yourself a favour lad and don't leave all those stones lying around in the road, we don't want the local idiots chucking them through the shop windows do we.'

Well thanks for that Sarge, I would never have worked that out for myself I thought. The van moved off leaving me stood on the street corner of the rapidly emptying town centre. No point in going back to the taxi office now, it was approaching 2am and I was due to walk back to the nick for my meal break. By the time I'd picked up all the cobblestones the town was much quieter, almost back to normal.

Back at the nick the same sergeant was already in the canteen, along with another four members of my team.

'Well, that wasn't too bad for a Christmas Eve,' suggested Richard. 'It's usually busier than that, suppose that it's been fairly quiet tonight.' Then he turned to me and asked, 'Has it been quiet in town Dave? It seemed steady enough when we drove through.'

I couldn't quite believe what I was hearing, I just looked at him, didn't say a word, but what I really wanted to say was:

NO IT WASN'T BLOODY QUIET. IT'S BEEN HELL OUT THERE AND ANOTHER THING THAT YOU LOT DON'T KNOW ABOUT, I NEARLY HAD TO DELIVER A BABY TONIGHT AND I'VE NEVER BEEN SO FRIGHTENED IN ALL MY LIFE.

No, I'd better keep such thoughts to myself, after all what was there to worry about? No one cared that I was only minutes away from becoming a midwife. Then, half an hour later, I stood and watched as a mob of thirty drunken thugs tried to crush each other's skulls with cobblestones. Just another quiet night on foot patrol in Brighouse town centre! Roll on New Year's Eve.

CHAPTER 4

Old Dogs, New Tricks

Charlie cut an imposing figure. He stood at well over six feet tall with silver hair and a neatly trimmed goatee beard, but he was still in good shape for a bloke in his early fifties. When on foot patrol he wore the old fashioned police cape draped around his shoulders, a throwback from the days of Dixon of Dock Green. And with less than two years to go before his retirement he was with me, pounding the beat in Brighouse town centre. Knowing nothing of his history, I did wonder about this strange turn of events. Just after ten o'clock we left the nick together, making our way into town where we'd get the chance for a proper natter, and I was sure that Charlie would spill the beans. His sudden transfer to Brighouse, he told me, was his punishment for what he described as a slight misdemeanor, a punishment dished out by the Chief Superintendent at Halifax.

I was still in probation, the start of my second year in the job and, compared to Charlie, had much to learn. More significantly, unlike him, I was not yet familiar with the politics and personal vendettas that exist within an organization like the police. The result of Charlie's disagreement with his boss was that tonight he was back pounding the beat. I wasn't quite sure if Charlie was supposed to be looking after me, or maybe our sergeant thought it was the other way round and I should be looking out for him. After all, there had been considerable change in the job since Charlie last wore a tall hat and took to the streets. And if I had learnt anything in the past year, it was that Saturday nights in Brighouse usually meant dealing with obnoxious drunks.

Walking along Bradford Road, I gave my new partner the benefit of my limited experience by stating the obvious; that drunken idiots rarely 'kick-off' before chucking out time, and that's usually after 11.30. So we'd have the first hour to wander around town, have a friendly chat and get to know each other.

The first thing that struck me about this veteran copper was his openness; he held nothing back and gave a detailed account of his fall from grace. It started, he admitted, with that slight disagreement with the Chief Superintendent, and the fact that Charlie was now walking the beat suggested that on this occasion he came out second best.

As his tale unfolded Charlie revealed that for the previous ten years he had been the Warrant Officer, his responsibility being to execute any warrants issued by the town's magistrates. He would track down, and if necessary arrest the miscreants who skipped bail or failed to pay any fines imposed by the courts. Charlie was in effect his own boss, he arranged his own work schedule and as long as the job was done efficiently he was left alone to get on with it.

We wandered around the town as Charlie explained his disagreement with the Chief Superintendent. It was all down to a claim for travelling expenses. He often used his own car for transport, usually when there wasn't an unmarked police car available. On those days he'd drive between the various courts or the police cells, or the known haunts of people wanted on warrant. Unfortunately for Charlie that's what turned out to be his downfall. When using his own car he quite rightly claimed a mileage allowance on his monthly expenses, but being a practical sort of bloke he had little time for unnecessary paperwork and didn't always keep accurate records.

His boss resented such autonomy and decided to bring Charlie to book. During a meeting that followed a blazing row ensued, which became personal when the Chief Super informed Charlie that he didn't like police officers with beards. Charlie was no shrinking violet and he replied, 'Well I don't like short, fat middle-aged police officers who have a hairstyle with a centre parting,' a description which just happened to fit the Chief Super.

The Division's most senior officer couldn't tolerate such insubordination; he literally blew his top and ordered Charlie out of the office. Charlie knew that he'd overstepped the mark but he walked out of that office with a smile on his face. However, by the following day Charlie was no longer the warrant officer at Halifax, instead he was here with me, walking the beat at Brighouse on a wet Saturday night. It just goes to show where the real power lies when a Chief Superintendent and a lowly constable have a slight difference of opinion.

It was an amusing and enlightening tale which Charlie finished telling just as we completed our first circuit of the town centre. Our foot patrol had taken us past the half dozen pubs, the two working men's clubs and a handful of restaurants and takeaways. The private hire taxi office was starting to fill up, a sure sign that our busy period would soon be upon us. I would soon see how Charlie's methods of dealing with the loud-mouthed drunks differed from my own. For over twelve months I'd patrolled this town but it was very different for Charlie. He last walked a foot beat in the good old days before the introduction of police radios. In Charlie's era of pounding the beat coppers really were on their own. If they came across a situation where they needed help then the only way to call for assistance would be a hearty blow on their police whistle, and the hope that a colleague happened to be within earshot. We were from completely different generations of policing, and I suspected we would have a different approach to the job.

We passed through the deserted bus station on our way towards the main shopping streets. Around the corner in Commercial Street was the nearest of the town centre pubs. Our first challenge of the night had just staggered out and it looked like he was heading our way. This particular young man was known to me, and as usual he was determined to make a nuisance of himself. 'Boylie' was his nickname, one of the regulars in and around the town centre at weekends.

When sober, Boylie could be quite amiable with patrolling officers but his attitude changed when drunk, especially in the presence of his mates. Then he became offensive and obnoxious and pushed his luck right to the very limit, but always stopping short of getting himself arrested. I had dealt him many times before when in a similar state so I knew what to expect. My usual approach was to try to humour him, maybe share some banter and persuade him to behave himself and go home quietly, but tonight things would be different. He was meeting Charlie for the first time.

'Evening officers,' said Boylie, the usual cheeky grin on his rosy face. He recognised me, nodded in my direction and then the banter started.

'Now then PC Watson, I see you're taking your granddad out for a walk tonight.'

I smiled back and tried to ignore the obvious insult but Boylie was on a roll and performing to the sniggering crowd behind him.

'Where did you find this old bloke then PC Watson? Down at the old folks' home was it?'

I sensed that Charlie didn't appreciate that jokey comment in the way that Boylie's vocal mates seemed to do, instead he was offended by this drunken youth and wasted little time in throwing down a verbal challenge. But I was still slightly taken aback when Charlie stepped forward so aggressively and leaned towards Boylie, his anger clearly visible, well at least it was for anyone sober enough to notice it.

'Don't you call me granddad again SUNSHINE, or I'll show you exactly what this granddad can do.'

Bloody hell, this bloke's on a short fuse I thought. Maybe I had just seen how Charlie's methods of dealing with drunks differed to mine. He was certainly more direct and forceful than me. I stood back and watched. This was going to be an interesting confrontation.

Boylie was not to be put off, he had his drunken audience behind him, half a dozen mates leaning against the window of the Indian restaurant, laughing at this exchange between their hero and the ancient copper he faced. The drunken oaf was in his element, determined to put on a show, and couldn't resist the chance to provide even further entertainment for his mates by humiliating Charlie. He slowly nodded his head, smirking and happy to be taunting this old copper.

'Come on then granddad, come on then, don't be shy, why don't you show us what you can do then granddad?'

Then the silly lad suddenly became much more animated, started bouncing up and down on the balls of his feet, both hands clenched into tight fists, pretending that Charlie was his sparring partner in a make-believe boxing match. He was playing to the crowd, dancing forward a little closer to throw a punch towards Charlie's face. There was obviously no real intent to strike a police officer, he was just showing off, but his mates cheered as the punch fell about two feet short of Charlie's chin. Boylie then darted back to more boisterous shouts from his fans. He was just messing with Charlie, quite prepared to poke fun at this very mature officer. But unfortunately for him, he didn't yet know what he was letting himself in for; and crucially, he didn't know that Charlie was patiently biding his time. Charlie had probably dealt with lads like this hundreds of times before, so he was ready and waiting with his clenched fist hidden inside the folds of his police cape.

The very next time that Boylie danced forward to throw another mock punch Charlie was prepared. With a quick twist of his upper body the front of his cape suddenly flew open. At the same time he lunged forward and his right fist appeared from nowhere. That tightly clenched fist flew out like a bolt of lightning and poor Boylie never even saw it coming. The thunderous blow crashed straight into his chin. It was a perfectly timed and crunching blow. Boylie's little dance forward was suddenly thrown into reverse. His head snapped back and his feet literally left the ground.

It all happened so quickly that I couldn't quite believe it myself. Boylie was thrown backwards into the road. He landed in the middle of a large puddle and tried to prop himself up on his elbows. In the background his mates were now silent, probably expecting some sort of response. But this time Boylie was too stunned to respond, and as for me, I was as surprised as they were. I looked aghast at Charlie, but his face was completely impassive. Now he stepped purposely towards his victim. I feared for Boylie and what was about to happen. I was almost too afraid to watch, half expecting that a kick to the ribs would follow. But that didn't happen, for Charlie the problem had been resolved. He took two more strides, then his third was a big stride right across Boylie's prostate body.

Almost mid-stride, Charlie paused for a moment and looked down at the drunken youth sprawled out beneath him. Then I heard the immortal words: 'And let that be a lesson to you Sunshine.' At the same time Charlie brushed the palms of his hands together, like he was treating this young pup with complete contempt, and then he just carried on walking. It was like a scene from a Clint Eastwood movie. I'd never seen anything quite like it before, surely Charlie was the inspiration for Dirty Harry.

He didn't hang about to admire his handiwork, instead he marched off along Bradford Road leaving Boylie sat in the puddle. The whole incident left me speechless. I'd always been told that if a copper uses force on anyone then he had a duty to make an arrest. Only by making an arrest could the 'use of force' be justified. Charlie could certainly show good cause to arrest Boylie, but, as I'd just witnessed, it wasn't his way. He couldn't be bothered with all the paperwork that an arrest would entail, and he'd made his point perfectly clear already.

For a full thirty seconds I stood and stared, rooted to the spot before hurrying after Charlie. On looking back I saw Boylie's mates gather around him. They picked him up off the ground and dusted him down. On this occasion, and for the first time that I could ever recall, there was no banter, no-one daring to take the mickey or carry on in their usual manner. Boylie and his crowd had all learned a lesson that night. And perhaps I had too; I'd seen how coppers patrolled the streets twenty years ago, before the introduction of the police radio.

Charlie's time with us was far too short as far as I was concerned. I thoroughly enjoyed my time working with him and seeing how policing was done in the fifties and sixties. Within a few short months he was reinstated in his old job at Halifax. An inquiry into his expenses had been conducted and, as expected, he was completely exonerated. He could now walk back into his old office with his head held high, and maybe he left some of his former colleagues at Brighouse a little wiser too.

CHAPTER 5

Miners' Strike

We climbed into the back of the van for the journey to Wakefield, five men to each side, all packed in like sardines on two inward facing benches. The plastic riot shields wedged into the far corner would be our only protection against the expected bricks and stones likely to come our way later in the day. Shoved under the seats, or held between cramped feet were our Nato riot helmets. Taking up the rest of the space were the blue canvas bags containing spare uniforms and equipment, all tightly packed into every nook and cranny. The prospect of another day in the back of this cold tin box didn't fill any of us with joy. Up front sat Mick, our driver for the day, a traffic cop when not driving the van on Police Support Unit (PSU) duties. Alongside him was Geoff Sefton, our burly sergeant squeezed into the ridiculously narrow middle seat; and to his left sat our inspector, the only bloke with the luxury of space to stretch out his legs. It was snowing heavily and the mood in the van was gloomy.

It was February 1985, the eleventh month of the miners' strike and we were all feeling the strain. Those awful early starts had become the norm. At 3.30am the alarm clock jolted me out of bed. First job was an early morning shower, hoping to wash away the tiredness. Then on with the uniform before creeping silently downstairs for a quick brew. Ten minutes later I was in the car for a 5-mile drive to Brighouse. Once there, subdued activity seemed to be the order of the day, a dozen men dashing about the nick collecting uniforms, riot shields, helmets and other equipment; and shoving it all into the van. That left just about enough time to climb aboard and hit the road; and all before 4.30am, little wonder that everyone was so miserable, all of us wondering what today held in store and at which pit would we face the heaving picket line. After eleven long months we all knew the score. We knew that the level of aggression differed greatly from one pit to the next but we wouldn't know our destination until after briefing. First, we were heading for Bishopgarth in Wakefield, West Yorkshire Police's training centre. The miners' strike dictated that training had just about stopped and Bishopgarth was now the new nerve centre of police operations.

During the 30-minute drive to Wakefield some of the lads were already halfway to nodding off, others were more pensive and sat quietly, heads leaning back against the metal grills covering the windows. A couple enjoyed an early morning fag, filling the van with their choking fumes. No real conversation took place, everyone was in their own little world, each one of us tired after working long shifts of thirteen or sometimes fourteen hours a day; and it had been like this for months.

There was a solemn silence in the van until I spoke. 'I'm going to become a dad,' I quietly announced, not really expecting any response from a group of exhausted coppers, but what the hell, I wanted to tell them anyway. Half a dozen heads slowly turned to face me. Pete looked up from his snooze and a smile spread across his sleepy face. His right hand reached towards me for a congratulatory hand shake.

'You kept that one a secret,' he mumbled, sleep deprivation slurring his words.

'Only found out myself last night,' I replied.

One by one they all went through the same ritual, including the sergeant and inspector until the mood in the van was surprising jovial, well at least it was for a few minutes until silence returned.

Shortly before 5am we were pulling into the parking area at Wakefield, already a scene of hectic activity, dozens of other PSU vans were already there. There were coppers from every nick in the force, many with the van doors wide open and men milling about outside. Some vans had already moved off, their briefing done and now en route to their designated pit. We found a space and parked up amongst the remaining vans, then clambered out into the darkness. We trudged towards the lights of the gymnasium for the day's briefing. The snow had stopped and instead there was a light drizzle but it was still bitterly cold. With my collar pulled up I walked with my head bowed down. I think that I preferred the snow.

Inside, the building was pleasantly warm and brightly lit. Over a hundred men in there, killing time or passing through or simply waiting for orders, which really meant that no one had yet decided where they would be going. It was like this every morning. Ordinary coppers like me were at the bottom of the command chain, which left me feeling that everything was haphazard and disorganised. But somehow things usually worked out in the end so I guess that someone must have known what they were doing, it just didn't feel that way.

Dozens of coppers sat around on the floor. Some played cards using a plastic riot shield as a makeshift table. A few were fast asleep, exhausted and sprawled out on the hard floor or long wooden benches. One or two hardy souls were using the gym equipment for a spot of personal keep fit or body building, but most just sat on the floor and leaned back against the wall to await their fate. No rest for our sergeant and inspector though, they were ushered straight over to the commanding officer's table and handed their instructions for the day. I crashed out on the floor alongside the rest of my PSU, not knowing how long we would be there.

A large TV blared out over in the corner showing the early morning news but no one took any notice. Everyone was too tired, or in a few cases, too busy to care about the outside world. I leaned my head back and closed my tired eyes, wanting to sleep, but thoughts of imminent fatherhood dominated. Our baby would be due in September and I wondered when the strike would be over and my life would get back to normal; or would things still be as they are now? On working days I usually went home just to sleep and eat and get cleaned up before the start of the next shift.

Geoff's voice startled me. 'Right lads, van up,' he ordered. I opened my eyes, not quite sure if I'd slept or not. 'We're off to Prince a' Wales at Ponte,' he announced. To the uninitiated that translated as, 'We're going to the Prince of Wales Colliery at Pontefract.' Reluctantly, we got to our feet, time to leave the relative warmth of the gymnasium and trudge back to the van. Dawn would soon be breaking, and thankfully the rain had stopped. Not yet 5.30, people with normal jobs would be still tucked up in bed. We climbed back into the van and left the doors wide open, allowing the cigarette smoke to waft out. We waited, the engine ticking over but the heater only warming the legs of those lucky enough to be sat in the front seats. A few minutes later Tony arrived back at the van after making his usual visit to the canteen. He now carried a plastic bread tray containing our sustenance for the next twelve hours in individual brown paper bags. They were affectionately known as 'doggy bags' and were distributed to eager hands before Tony scurried off again to return the empty bread tray to the canteen. Rummaging through those doggy bag was one of the day's highlights, although I don't really know why as they contained the worst food imaginable. I delved into the mysterious contents: a pork pie wrapped in cellophane, the manufacturer's name unknown to me, but usually consisting of stale pastry surrounding a ball of fat and gristle; the usual two sandwiches, a cheese slice on one and a single slice of wafer thin ham in the other; then a chunk of fruit cake, also wrapped in cellophane; to bulk up the bag there was the obligatory bag of crisps, again an unknown brand; and finally a Mars bar. Drinks for the day consisted of one can of fizzy orange juice. How appetizing, what more could a man possibly want to sustain himself for a hard day of pushing and shoving against aggressive miners?

Tony was back from the canteen, he climbed in the van and we were off, driving through the streets of Wakefield, all of us now wide awake and grumbling about the contents of our doggy bags, each one slightly different but all of them equally dreadful. Within minutes, someone opened the rear doors whilst we were still moving. Seconds later a barrage of sausage rolls and pork pies were hurled out, last seen bouncing along the tarmac in every direction. How many of the other vans have just done exactly that I wondered, it had become something of a ritual. The main road through the city centre was now littered with dozens of discarded pies and sausage rolls, our way of showing contempt for the garbage packed into those doggy bags.

Half an hour later we arrived at the gates of the Prince of Wales Colliery. More than a dozen police vans were already there, parked up in a neat row with their back doors wide open, coppers sitting inside and waiting for the next command. We parked up alongside to join in the waiting game. Our inspector and sergeant walked away for yet another briefing. I tried to sleep but the temperature was far too cold for that.

Some time later, I don't know how long, Geoff returned. He announced that the working miners, all four of them, would be brought to the pit at 7am. They would be in two separate vans and would travel in convoy, one police van would lead the convoy with another bringing up the rear. Four vans in total. Didn't seem logical to me to use so many vans for so few miners, but who was I to question the order.

By 6.45am we were ready for action, out of the van and forming a police line across the width of the colliery road, ordinary uniforms only, not a riot shield or Nato helmet in sight. Apparently a spokesman for the NUM thought it made us look too aggressive and wouldn't be good for public relations. We stood in line three deep, our commanding officers standing resolutely behind us. In front gathered a hundred striking miners, peaceful and relatively quiet for the moment. Off to one side of the pickets were a couple of braziers, ironically both of them glowing bright red with a generous supply of coal. The warmth from the braziers was inviting on such a cold morning, but obviously out of bounds for us. A home-made placard propped against the fence declared that: 'Miners United Will Never be Defeated'. In the distance an army of pickets marched towards us, scores, perhaps hundreds of men chanting their mantra and raising their banners in unison. It was another determined show of solidarity. But all this was to save face. No more than a final act of defiance because everyone knew that these men were already defeated, it would be only a matter of time before they went back to the coalface, or failing that, joined the dole queue.

We squeezed into the police line where I was unfortunate enough to be stuck on the front row, the one place where the unstoppable force usually met the immovable object. The very place where you were most likely to feel a steel toe-capped boot smash into your shins, or if you were really unlucky, feel the bones in your face break when half a house brick came to a painful stop; and of course when the big push starts it's here that you'd have the breath squeezed from your lungs by men pushing from both directions.

In the distance the small convoy of vans headed towards us. A police Transit van led the way, wire grills covering the windows and blue lights flashing. Following closely behind were two more Transit vans, white in colour, and the hire company's name boldly painted on the side panels. Bringing up the rear is another police van, again with blue lights on and grills over the windows. This is not a high-speed convoy, too many pickets for that, all four vans moving at a steady speed past the shouting and jeering miners. An occasional brick or clod of earth takes to the air, the thrower un-identifiable. Less than 200 yards to go before our line will swing open from the centre like the two halves of double electric gates, but only long enough for the convoy to pass through before snapping shut again to hold back the army of striking miners.

There was tension in the air, hundreds of agitated pickets only yards away but not yet paying us any attention, more concerned about showing their anger and bitter hatred towards the few desperate and frightened miners hiding in the vans and daring to break the strike. As the convoy gets closer the volley of bricks increased but still the vans kept moving.

On the opposite side of the road to the colliery lies Pontefract Racecourse, a vast expanse of open ground, so huge that it's virtually impossible to police. The pickets, of course, are prepared to use this open space to their advantage, something they'd been doing in recent days. A score of men had already climbed over the dense thorn hedge and now waited on the racecourse. From there they could freely throw stones and clods of earth at the convoy of vans or the lines of police without fear of retribution. They didn't yet know it, but this was the last day to enjoy such freedom of movement. Today our commanding officer had made provisions to deal with such tactics.

In the distance, and too far away to be seen by the naked eye, were six mounted police officers sitting astride their horses, all fully equipped in protective riot gear, and purposely kept out of sight. Then, minutes later when the stones started flying a radio message was sent from our commanding officer. He ordered those mounted officers into action in what was a carefully planned operation. Moving off at a canter, they came round from the far side of the racecourse. A minute later I saw them for the first time and watched in fascination as they spread out across the full width of the straight, six abreast, and increasing their speed to a gallop. From my biased perspective it was an impressive sight, six mounted officers on their huge horses charging down the racecourse with their heavy truncheons drawn and held high above their heads, Ready to bring their weapons down to strike any stone-throwing pickets who dared to stand in their way.

The stone throwers were less impressed. Six mounted gladiators bearing down on them must have been bloody terrifying! The roles were instantly reversed, the violent pickets were no longer a threat to a few frightened 'scabs'. This small group of pickets were now definitely the underdogs, with nothing but the odd stone or a clod of earth to protect themselves. The result was instant panic. They tried to flee by vaulting over, or sometimes charging, straight through the prickly thorn hedge, desperate for the protection of their fellow pickets. But even that contingency had been planned for by our diligent commanding officer. He'd seen the tactics used by these pickets all too often so this time there would be no easy escape. Instead, he ordered several dog handlers to be strategically positioned. They laid in wait, hidden on the other side the hedge, the police dogs held on long tethers to be simultaneously given their freedom to do what they do best; that is to attack anyone who takes them by surprise when vaulting over the hedge.

It must have been a terrible dilemma for the stone throwers, either face being charged down by a line of mounted police officers, or choose the bared and vicious teeth of the police dogs. To a man, and I could understand why, they all chose the dogs. Some were lucky and escaped back into the throng of their fellow pickets, but others laid screaming on the ground with a snarling Alsatian hanging onto an arm or a leg. From the police lines came a triumphant cheer.

For the majority of men that one incident was little more than a minor distraction, an entertaining side show, but it would not prevent the main business of the day. Our job was to make sure that the working miners, or scabs as the pickets called them, were able to pass safely through the picket lines. On the other hand, the hundreds of massed pickets considered that their job was to stop them. And they intended to do so by any means whatsoever, including the use of violence.

The convoy of vans was now almost upon us, and like a well-oiled machine our uniformed barricade opened up to let them through before snapping shut again to provide a human barrier. Immediately the pickets began to surge forward, hundreds of men leaning into each other and pushing for all they were worth. The men facing us weren't the usual Saturday night drunks that I was accustomed to dealing with, they weren't the young men about town who were often little more than teenagers with too much beer inside them. This time we were up against men who were more mature, sober, but still aggressive, physically strong and tough men who were used to hard manual work. And they believed that they had a cause worth fighting for; it was about the future of their jobs and the very survival of their communities.

I found myself pushing against one such man, both of us locked into the struggle by the heaving masses all around us, neither of us able to move to the left or the right. We stumbled first backwards and then forwards, face to face in a crazy, heaving and exhausting dance. He was an older man, about thirty years my senior, puffing and panting with the exertion. Gave me the impression that he didn't want to be there anymore than I did.

'Haven't you got owt better to do than this?' I asked, hoping that he would choose to talk rather than deliver a kick or a punch.

'Plenty,' he replied. 'Not much choice though have I really.'

The big push continued for a few more minutes until the scabs were safely out of sight, only then did the heaving begin to ease. The pickets had made their point, but as usual it was all in vain. The strike breakers still got through the picket line, even if it was with the help of 'Maggie's Army'.

In the minutes that followed many of the pickets started to melt away, they would be back again when the scabs were due to leave the pit at the end of their shift. That would be another eight hours away but I knew that we'd still be there, waiting for the pickets to return. On the television news this evening the National Coal Board (NCB) would again falsely claim that the strike was crumbling and that this pit was being worked, but I knew differently, four frightened strike breakers wouldn't be digging much coal.

At last I could breath more easily, the pressure of hundreds of men pushing against each other was over for now. But my adversary from the big push was still there, leaning forward with hands resting on knees, taking a breather. I was intrigued by what he said earlier, so I decided to speak to him again.

'Oi, fella, what did you mean back then?' I asked. 'When you said that you'd no choice but to be here.'

He straightened up and took a couple of paces towards me, wanting to speak confidentially and out of earshot of his fellow miners.

'I don't want to be out on strike lad,' he told me. 'I never did, should have retired over six months ago but they won't let me retire when I'm out on strike, and if I go through that picket line, like those scabs, my life won't be worth living.'

And with that he turned and walked away. Leaving me with much to think about. A bloke of his age probably had

kids who were older than me. If he had sons then they were
also likely to work down the pit. All their livelihoods
were threatened with the pit closures. Unbeknown to any
of my colleagues, and but for a twist of fate, I could so easily
be stood alongside that bloke rather than opposing him.
In recent months I'd researched my own family tree. The
results confirmed that my mother's family came from a
mining community not ten miles from where I now stood.
My research was made easier because of that mining connection. Generation after generation of my ancestors had
followed the same path. A boy would be born into a mining
village, after leaving school he would start his working life
down the pit. By the time that he was in his early twenties he
would usually marry a local girl, they would have a family
and any sons would follow the same pathway. I traced my
ancestors all the way back to the early 1800s, and just about
every male on the census records had 'coal miner' shown
as the occupation. In my family's case the break with that
tradition came with my mother's generation, most of her
siblings happened to be girls and for them there was little
work in the coal mining area. Her father's health was poor so
they left the pit village and moved the thirty or so miles to
Bradford. This was in the 1930s when work was plentiful for
girls in the booming textile mills in and around Bradford.

As a child I often visited the mining area around Barnsley.
I would travel by bus from Bradford during the school
holidays and stay with relatives where I made new friends
with the local kids. I remembered days of wandering around
the lanes and fields with other lads, making fun of their
strange accent and enjoying the closeness of the mining
communities.

So I now felt torn by what was happening around me.
I understood what these miners were fighting for, and I
believed that the Conservative Government were cynically
using the police as a political tool to destroy trade unions. I
also resented some of the antics used by a few of my fellow
police officers towards the pickets to humiliate them. On
more than one occasion I had seen officers openly displaying
their monthly pay slip, holding it proudly above their heads

to be read by destitute miners. It was a disgraceful gesture carried out by a minority of officers earning hundreds of pounds a month in overtime, when at the same time the striking miners were going without.

Within an hour the mass of striking miners had left the picket line to return home. Only a few remained, they stood around the braziers to maintain the official picket line. Now that the threat to the strike breakers was gone we climbed back into the van to sit and wait, and then we waited some more. What followed was many hours of doing nothing but sitting around. Games of cards were popular and the mood was fairly light-hearted, fortunately no reported injuries on the day. It was a different story yesterday when Alan from our PSU took a brick in the mouth, his face unprotected because the powers-that-be won't usually allow us to wear our Nato helmets with their protective visors, looks too aggressive, they say. I say try telling that to Alan with his stitched lips and smashed teeth. But today was a good day. The gaffer's plan with the mounted officers and dogs worked a treat so maybe we could expect less trouble at this pit from now on.

My colleagues enjoy their moment of victory. But I see things slightly differently. I don't like to dampen the mood so I keep my thoughts to myself. In a moment of quiet contemplation I think back to last week when we were working at another, much smaller pit. I can't keep track of them all but I believe it was Acton Hall Colliery. On that night the police definitely lost, and it proved to be rather embarrassing. The night started out looking very promising because we were at one of the less hostile pits. We arrived there during the evening and formed the usual police lines to provide the handful of working miners a safe exit. Then we retired to the works canteen for what should have been a quiet night.

With no more activity expected until the following morning we hoped to have a good sleep. The morning's scabs should arrive about 7am and again they would be hidden in the back of a Transit van. Our job would be to get them through the picket line before escorting them into this very room. Then we'd stay with them until our relief from the

PSU on the day shift arrived from Wakefield. That would be the end of our shift and time for us to go home.

All had been going well, or so we thought from the comfort and safely of the canteen. Many of us used the time for a well deserved sleep, grateful to have a cushy number for a change. Then at about 5am all hell broke loose when the pit deputy burst in, looking very agitated and worried. He had been forced to abandon his car almost half a mile away and make his way on foot. The access road, he told us, was now completely blocked: whilst we slept some enterprising pickets had been busy with a chain saw and several large trees had been expertly felled. Those trees now lay across the full width of the access road leading to the pit. So the nocturnal activities of the unknown lumberjacks had ensured that there would be no scabs at work today. A handful of pickets, armed with nothing more than a chainsaw, had achieved what hundreds of their fellow miners had failed to do for weeks. This time they had definitely stopped the scabs getting through. And now it would take hours to clear the road. Only then could we drive away with our tails between our legs. On that day it was the turn of the pickets to have a laugh at our expense.

In another month the strike would be over, the miners would be defeated but there were no real winners. In my humble opinion, for what it's worth, there would be only losers, and the greatest losers were the mining communities of the Yorkshire coalfield. I felt guilty, knowing that my own future was fairly secure in the police force. It would be easy for me to pick up the pieces and move on with my life, but for the men who I had struggled against for almost a year such a transition would be almost impossible.

CHAPTER 6

Keeping Up Appearances

Bank holidays mean two things to most coppers; the first is that if you happen to be working you will receive double pay; second, those who are working will be short-staffed because half of the team will be at home on bank holiday leave.

That was the situation for a night shift on Boxing Day in the mid 1980s. I was the driver of the public order van, patrolling in the Ford Transit, enough room in the back for a dozen coppers but no such luck this time. Tonight I would have a crew of just two trusty colleagues, John Gill and Anne Holiday, both very inexperienced and still in their probationary period. So with five years' service behind me I was the old sweat of the team and I would be expected to take charge at any awkward jobs.

It was nearly midnight when we were sent to our next job, an incident taking place in a pub on the edge of a council estate. We left the town centre for the short drive of only a mile or so. Control kept the information coming; there was a disco taking place and the pub was packed to the rafters. Unusually for this pub, the landlord had decided to charge for admission, but two of the regulars had refused to pay. Instead they pushed straight past him and walked right up to the bar. They were now downing their pints, but the landlord wanted them thrown out.

Incidents like this were fairly common at some pubs, especially on bank holidays. It didn't sound like much of a problem, well not until Control added that one of the men involved happened to be Eric Burnley. Oh hell, that's the last thing we needed. That very name was enough to put the fear of God into most coppers, including me. Burnley was reputedly the 'hardest bloke in town', a powerfully-built man with an inbuilt hatred of the police; and known to be capable of extreme violence when drunk.

Suddenly I was envious of the colleagues who were enjoying their night off. We drove in tense silence on the short drive to the pub. Burnley was not a man to confront when we were so short-staffed. Now feeling really nervous, I pulled on to the car park and brought the van to a stop right outside the front door, intending that the vehicle was seen by everyone inside; and secretly hoping that Burnley would think that we had extra coppers tucked away in the back should he kick off and we needed help. I warned John and Anne about Burnley and his violent past. Sensibly, they both hung back as we walked towards the open door of the pub. The landlord stood waiting for us, a middle-aged, skinny little man with a droopy moustache and glasses. Not what I had hoped for. On a night like this what we really needed was a big 20-stone bruiser, but clearly it wasn't to be. If there was trouble this little weed of a landlord would be next to useless.

I entered the rowdy pub and glanced across towards Burnley who stood at the bar. He looked straight at me and spoke briefly to his cousin. They were easy enough to pick out, the pair of them were easily the biggest blokes in there. The disco was in full swing, or at least it was until three uniformed coppers walked in; then we suddenly became the evening's live entertainment. The DJ saw us approach the bar and sensing trouble the music was discreetly turned off. Everyone suddenly stopped what they were doing and turned to watch. Surely these coppers wouldn't dare to come in here to arrest Eric Burnley; or if they were stupid enough to try then it would be fun watching.

The landlord marched the few paces towards the bar and quickly fulfilled his legal obligation by telling his unwelcome guests that they had to leave the premises. The little man then quickly took two steps backwards and left me to carry out his dirty work. On nights like this I'd rather be having a beer than having to chuck out the hardest man in town. There was no immediate reaction from Burnley. Fortunately his cousin appeared much less threatening, although he too was a huge man, even taller than Burnley. He looked like he must be the strong silent type which was fine with me. The giant stood with his back to us, quietly leaning on the bar and swallowing his beer in great gulps. Burnley on the other hand was in his usual antagonistic mood, and tonight I was sure that he was spoiling for a fight, one that he would no doubt win.

The two of us stood facing each other, about a yard apart. He was about the same age as me, and similar height but about four stone heavier, and all of it solid muscle. I was no threat to him, and he knew it. He raised his glass from the bar and took a long swig of his beer, his eyes never leaving mine as he carefully placed the glass back on the bar before speaking.

'Oh aye, and what are you gonna do if I don't leave?'

Oh bloody hell, I could do without this. He'd thrown down the gauntlet and now waited to see if I had the nerve to pick it up. Why do jobs like this always happen on a bank holiday when we are so short-staffed? My colleagues sensibly stayed just behind me. I consoled myself with the thought that if Burnley did thump me at least they'd be there to catch me before I hit the deck. I really was quaking in my boots, convinced that he could see me shaking, nearly peeing my pants now, but trying to appear confident, even though I didn't feel it! He waited for me to answer, better make this sound good Dave, I said to myself.

'Well Eric, you heard the landlord, he wants you out of here, so I'm telling you that you're leaving, whether you like it or not. Why don't you just walk away whilst you've still got some dignity left?'

He picked up his beer, smiled at me and slowly nodded his head back and forth, then he took another mouthful of beer before placing his glass on the bar. Again he looked at me but still didn't reply, a confident grin on his face, it was my move. I tried again but I was running out of options. 'Eric if you refuse to leave we'll get a van full of men here, we'll lock you up and drag you out in handcuffs.' I was desperately hoping that he would agree to my pathetic demand so I finished by saying, 'And then you'll be spending the rest of the night in our cells.'

I was bluffing but I'd done my best, tried to sound convincing, but it looked like I'd failed miserably. Burnley was unmoved and obviously in no hurry to leave. Instead he calmly picked up his pint from the bar, his meaty fist wrapped firmly around the base of the glass. A horrible thought suddenly occurred to me, was he holding the beer glass in that way so he could use it as a weapon? Now I really was scared, feared that he was going to shove it into my face.

How long would it take him? How long to ram that glass straight into my face? Less than a second I reckoned. I dare not blink; I saw nothing other than that beer glass. But I wouldn't go down without a fight. I stared at the 'weapon', watching for any sudden movement. At the same time I instinctively slid my right thumb through the leather thong of my truncheon. Got it, I wrapped my fingers tightly round the grip but left it, for now in its concealed pocket down the side of my right thigh. There was a silent standoff as Burnley calmly drank his beer. I thought about my chances of getting in the first strike. It would be a gamble, knocking him out with one single blow would be my only chance, a chance that I was prepared to take if that beer glass moved just one inch in my direction.

By now the whole pub was in relative silence, the clientele had become our audience, maybe a hundred people watching the incident evolve. The atmosphere was intense, could be cut with a knife; I didn't dare take my eyes off Burnley, not even for a split second. My heart was racing, my mouth dry and the arteries throbbing in my temples. Still I watched that beer glass, had to give the impression that I was in control so I concentrated on my breathing, trying to look calm and relaxed. The stand-off probably only lasted half a minute but to me it seemed like an eternity. Then Burnley finished his beer and slowly placed the empty glass back on the bar.

What a relief that was. Burnley obviously didn't feel the need for a weapon; I suppose I should be grateful for that if nothing else. If he was determined to fight then now would be the time. His face gave no clue to what he was thinking but was still menacing. He glared at me, trying to weigh me up, or maybe he was just testing me, almost taunting me. Perhaps he could see straight through my false bravado, could see the fear in my eyes and was enjoying it. Then just as my heart rate was up to a thousand beats a minute the hard stare became a smile when he said, 'Right then boys and girls, if I agree to leave this dump will you guys give me a lift home in your van?'

Give him a lift home in our van, bloody hell, I'd have been more than happy to carry him home on my back, I would push him home in a supermarket trolley if that's what he really wanted! I couldn't begin to put into words the sense of relief. I'd been convinced that we were going to get a severe beating in that pub, but not tonight. A moment later I walked out of the pub with my head held high, felt like I was floating across the ground rather than walking upon it. Burnley walked alongside me with John and Anne following behind. At the van I opened the doors and heard the music blaring out again, looked like the DJ would have to earn his fee tonight after all.

No doubt some of the punters were disappointed. There wasn't going to be a fight, maybe some of them were disappointed that the coppers didn't get a good hiding. The big, silent cousin decided to make his own way home. But Burnley, as always, wanted to maintain his tough guy image in the presence of his audience. He knew that the pub regulars were watching and insisted on taking the front passenger seat, and I didn't have the nerve to argue. My colleagues climbed into the back and sat on the wooden bench.

We left the pub car park and headed towards Burnley's house. He wanted to talk, asked me what I had planned for New Year's Eve and how my Christmas Day had gone, he was friendly and chatty. It had turned out to be a good result after all. I intended to drop Burnley off at his house and then carry on with our patrol. But as I brought the van to a stop outside his abode he turned to me with an invitation. 'Are you lot coming in for a drink then?' I hesitated, not really knowing how to answer. He wasn't to be put off. 'Come on fella, have a beer, let your hair down a bit,' he went on, 'It's still Christmas you know.'

I thought about his invitation for a whole two-seconds; if there was ever a time when I really needed a beer then this was it, I couldn't say no could I? The change in this man was quite incredible and as we were to discover, he turned out to be a fine host with three uniformed coppers sat in the tiny terraced house sharing his beer.

Only when we all had a beer in our hands did I really relax. Burnley apologized for his earlier conduct, offering the excuse that he had his reputation to think of in the pub. He told us that he resented the landlord for demanding admission money to the disco, especially when it was his local pub. I chose not to mention my own fears, and had it not been for keeping up appearances I would have gladly paid their admission money out of my own pocket. It was only 50p each, certainly not worth getting a good kicking for.

CHAPTER 7

Carry on Capers

It was hard to believe but, yes, we really did have a working brothel in the heart of Brighouse. Conveniently placed on the edge of the town centre, this establishment had been quietly going about its business for several months already. Obviously the place wasn't openly advertised as a brothel, to the uninitiated and the ignorant (like me) it was a perfectly legitimate business. Officially it was run as a massage parlour and nothing more, but we knew different. However, this was to be their last day of providing sexual gratification for some of the local male population. What I didn't yet know was that within a couple of hours our carefully planned raid would become such a farce that it could be a comedy sketch from one of the 'Carry On' movies.

Preparation for this day had been going on for weeks. First there had been the unmarked police observation van which was parked discreetly within sight of the 'Massage Parlour'. Hidden in the back of the van, and behind the blacked-out windows were two men from our 'Scenes of Crime Dept' (known as SOCO officers). For days now they had photographed every person entering or leaving the building. However, those photographs alone wouldn't be enough to secure any criminal convictions, so in an attempt to gather even more damning evidence a young fresh-faced officer was brought in from another police division. His dubious role was to visit the parlour whilst wearing civilian clothing and posing as a genuine paying customer. Once inside he was to make a mental note of the various activities and get to know the various people involved. He may have even sampled the 'extras' that the girls were offering in addition to a routine massage. It was all cloak and dagger stuff and not what I would normally expect to find in our civilised little town.

The day of the raid started off with a very formal briefing at Brighouse nick. Uniformed officers were there in force. There were representatives from various other departments such as the CID and SOCO and the Task Force; and of course numerous supervisory officers, all hoping to be in on the action. Over twenty people crammed into the compact briefing room and we were soon split up into small teams of three or four. Each team was given a specific responsibility; one of the main objectives, we were told, was to arrest the two men who owned and ran the brothel. Apparently these blokes were high-profile criminals and suspected of being involved in a series of robberies elsewhere in the country.

The working girls were to be arrested on suspicion of living off immoral earnings. Any paying customers would be given a choice: either provide a witness statement there and then, or if they refused to do so, be faced with the potential of a court summons popping through the letterbox.

So far so good, everything appeared to be going well. Although it was all new to me, it was clear that someone had spent many hours gathering all this information. On the walls of the briefing room hung display boards with mug shots of punters visiting the place in the last two weeks. Trade was clearly booming with almost forty such photographs. Some of them I recognised, many were local men who frequented the pubs or shopped in the town centre on a Friday or Saturday. Each of the teams was handed a pre-prepared evidence pack containing information about every suspect. Everything we could possibly need was included: the mug shots, detailed descriptions, times that they usually visited, their known associates and even the cars which they drove.

All seemed to be going smoothly until the man who would lead the raid walked into the room; unbelievably it was my own team inspector, Mad Harry Buttersby. And Harry was given that nickname for good reason, he was absolutely stark raving bonkers, and surely everyone in the Division knew that! Harry was not the sort of bloke who would excel in this role. I had to assume that the top man didn't know about our inspector's style of policing.

Clearly some of my colleagues were as shocked as I was at Harry's unexpected arrival, from somewhere behind me I heard the muffled sound of sniggering, and from my left I felt Andy playfully dig me in the ribs as Harry took his seat. Moments later calm was restored and the briefing continued. The observation van, we were told, was already in place and at least two male customers had been seen to enter the building in the last half hour. The detective who planned the raid continued, stressing the importance of securing evidence to prove that punters were paying the girls for 'extras'. To get this right, he told us, we needed to time the raid very carefully.

I listened with interest, now looking forward to what sounded like an exciting event rather than the usual eight hours of driving a panda car. With the briefing over we trudged outside and climbed into the back of two police vans, our transport to the brothel. Five minutes later we were on the other side of town with the vans parked up, only a short walk to reach our objective. And that's when everything started to go horribly wrong; Harry ordered us to line up in single file alongside the vans. It was like a military parade, with him taking on the role of a Drill Sergeant, and what a motley crew we must have looked. Our leader barked out his commands at the top of his voice. My understanding was that we were supposed to arrive at the brothel silently, hopefully for an element of surprise, but Harry was already drawing attention by shouting out his orders.

'We're not going to go in there like a rabble,' he bellowed. 'We'll go in, in an orderly fashion, now turn to your left and ... QUICK ... MARCH ... LEFT, RIGHT, LEFT, RIGHT.'

I don't know where Harry had been for the last twenty years but he clearly didn't know that the CID officers had long since forgotten how to march. Worse still, the SOCOs (photographers) weren't even police officers. They were civilian staff who had never set foot on a drill square in their life. But Harry didn't care about that; instead he insisted that we follow his orders. Like a military general he strode out and led from the front, proudly swinging out his arms and legs like a clockwork soldier. We were almost there but Harry was still barking out his commands: 'LEFT, RIGHT, LEFT, RIGHT, LEFT ...' I was towards the back of the raiding party but when I looked forward I found it impossible not to burst out laughing. Despite Harry's best intentions our pathetic line of plain clothes and uniformed men were making very little attempt to keep in formation. I was sure that such antics hadn't been part of the master plan, but maybe the top brass hadn't allowed for the idiosyncrasies of 'Mad Harry'. The raid was just starting and already things were falling apart.

We approached from the side of the building, a former industrial unit which until recently was run as a plumber's workshop and office. If there was ever a perfect place to run a brothel then this was probably it. There wasn't a house within sight, there were no schools or churches or other buildings where innocent members of the public could take offence. In that part of town a discreetly run brothel wasn't going to interfere with any other day-to-day activities.

Our disorderly march came to a stop outside the building. Now we were ready to enter en masse, still hoping for an element of surprise. Then, on Harry's command, we burst in through the front door. Inside, a woman sitting behind a desk looked up in surprise, her official job was presumably that of receptionist. She wore a very small bright red top which made a poor attempt to conceal very large boobs. Her mouth fell open on seeing twenty blokes charge straight in, many of them in police uniform. She held a telephone in her left hand but was suddenly stunned into silence.

Flashbulbs were going off as the SOCO expertly photographed her. One of our team escorted her outside so she could be questioned back at the nick. Meanwhile the rest of us continued straight through an internal door into the rear of the building. It led through to another room which was subdivided just like the plans had shown on the briefing. The undercover cop had obviously done a good job of memorizing the layout. To our left were three small cubicles, the first two were unoccupied, their doors left wide open to reveal a single massage table inside each room. Directly in front of us was a glass-fronted sauna. Inside there sat a solitary man who looked aghast when he saw us through the glass screen, he was completely naked. The poor fella couldn't believe his eyes on finding himself right in the middle of a police raid. He promptly picked up a newspaper and used it to cover his private parts, pretending to study the day's horse racing in the sports section.

Unfortunately I was teamed up with Harry (probably because no one else would work with him). The third member of our team was James, one of the SOCO photographers. Harry stomped straight up to the door of the last cubicle, the only one still closed; he tried the handle but it was locked from the inside. I was directly behind Harry but he had no intention of knocking on the door and waiting for a reply. He took one step backwards and nearly knocked me over before quickly regaining his balance and giving the door an almighty kick with the sole of his right boot. The flimsy barrier flew open and its feeble lock parted company from the woodwork, somersaulting into the air. Harry glanced inside, stepped to one side and bellowed at James a one word order:

'PHOTOGRAPH!'

There was now a real sense of urgency in his voice, sadly my view inside the room was completely blocked by the bulk of Harry, but he must have seen something of interest. James instantly darted forward into the doorway, already in the process of dropping down on to one knee. Like a true professional his camera was in position, the viewfinder pressed firmly against his right eye as he quickly squatted down to take the evidential picture.

So far everything had run like clockwork, but unfortunately all that was about to change. Harry had kicked open the door with such brute force that it swung back and crashed straight into the wall behind. But it was moving so quickly that it bounced off that wall before instantly swinging back to its closed position. All this happened at the exact same time as

James was about to take his first photograph. The closing door came hurtling towards the telephoto lens of his camera. The door crashed into the camera which was then shunted backwards into his face. The poor chap reacted like he'd been shot with a high-calibre rifle, nearly performing a backwards somersault and ending up in a heap on the floor. The camera was knocked from his grasp and sent spinning across the floor, and that was before he'd taken a single photograph.

It was all too much for me, I was in fits of uncontrollable laughter. Tears rolled down my cheeks and I covered my face in an attempt to hide my frivolity. Only then did I look inside the cubicle to see for myself the cause of Harry's sudden excitement. A middle-aged man was laid on his back on the massage table. He raised his head and looked towards the door only to see two uniformed coppers staring straight at him. This man was completely naked with his penis stood proudly to attention. Alongside him stood one of the girls, she was topless and I guess that she had been providing this customer with some 'extra services' rather than just a massage. The pair of them remained there open-mouthed and not knowing what to do. But at least our entry hadn't been captured on film. The injured SOCO officer was now laid in the doorway, groaning in pain and rolling around on the floor, openly cursing Harry and calling him every name under the sun. He was almost on the verge of tears as he rubbed his bruised eye; the poor lad's broken camera now discarded on the floor some distance behind him.

Finally some sort of order was restored. It transpired that the owners of the business were not on the premises after all.

Later that day the working girls and their clients all gave statements which included important evidence against the owners. Towards the end of the shift we returned to the police station for a formal debriefing and again everything sounded very professional. Our proud inspector took centre stage and suggested that the operation had been a complete success. I didn't see it quite the same way; my overriding impression was that it had been a memorable day, but for all the wrong reasons.

CHAPTER 8

Kermit the Frog

After seven happy years at Brighouse I was ready for a change of scenery. It was now 1988, over a year had passed since I had moved our family home from the suburbs of Bradford to a small town on the edge of the Yorkshire Dales. It was the perfect place to bring up a young family, but I soon found that the daily commute to Brighouse was both time consuming and expensive. Reluctantly I came to the conclusion that I needed a transfer to a police division which was closer to my new home.

Bradford North Division was to be my choice, an area of great variety and a new place for me to get to grips with. It's a division that includes all the towns in the northern part of the Aire Valley. A vacancy at Keighley was ideal, being the nearest town to the boundary with rural North Yorkshire and only a pleasant 15-minute drive from my home.

My new posting eventually came through but it wasn't Keighley after all. Instead I was heading to Manningham Sub Division, in the heart of Bradford, an inner city area and very different from Brighouse.

I moved in January 1989. My first week was working the night shifts at Manningham. After two rest days I was back on early turn shift which started at 6am. By mid-morning I was out on patrol somewhere in Bradford when I heard my call sign on the radio.

'Hotel Alpha 2, can you return to the station, the Superintendent wants to see you straight away.'

That was the full extent of the message. No further information was forthcoming and it left me wondering just

what he wanted. I was already a bit worried, as when a lowly
PC is ordered to see the big boss it's usually for a rollocking.
On the drive back to the nick I racked my brain, surely I
couldn't be in trouble already? I was puzzled, I had only
been at Manningham for just over a week and now I was
being told to go to the Super's office.

Ten minutes later I pulled into the car park, locked the car
and anxiously walked through to the main office. My new
inspector, together with the desk sergeant and the radio op
all looked up as I entered the room. They too probably
wondered why I had been instructed to see the top man. I
spoke to Inspector Holden, although I barely knew him but
first impressions were that he could be trusted.

'Do you know what this is about Boss?' I asked.

'No idea Dave,' he replied. 'Surely you're not in the brown
smelly stuff already?'

'Don't think so,' I answered.

'Well, you'll soon find out, just make sure you wear
your helmet, and don't forget to throw him one up when you
go in.'

It was my inspector's way of telling me to salute when
I entered the Super's office, nothing like creating a good
impression when meeting him for the first time. I left the
room and made for the stairs, the higher echelons are where
mere mortals such as I usually feared to tread. I continued
up, past the CID offices, then up again to the hallowed
ground occupied by the Chief Inspector and Superintendent.
I ventured forth, finally finding the nameplate of Superintendent Cable. I knocked and waited a few seconds. I was just
about to knock again when the command came. 'ENTER,'
he shouted. In I went, snapped to attention and saluted. He
remained sat behind his desk.

'Ah, PC Watson, take a seat,' he ordered.

I removed my helmet and sat with my back ramrod
straight on the chair facing his desk, seeing my new boss for
the first time. He was definitely younger than I expected,
barely forty I guessed, probably one of the high flyers on the
accelerated promotion scheme, one of those who was always
moving onwards and upwards every couple of years. Little

doubt that he was destined for higher things. Not the sort of bloke to be in charge of a run down nick like Queen's House at Manningham, I thought, too clean-cut for this sort of place; and maybe too highly educated.

He put down the paperwork he was reading and stared at me for several seconds.

'PC Watson. Do you know why you are here?' he finally asked.

'No Sir,' I answered, purposely keeping my response brief, reluctant to give anything away.

He had obviously played this game before and didn't want to reveal his hand just yet. 'Well then, tell me why YOU think you have been asked to come in and see me this morning.' He deliberately placed greater emphasis on the word 'you' as though he was expecting me to confess all my sins.

I hadn't exactly decided to 'come in to see him', I mused, a better description would be to say that I had been summoned to see him without any explanation being offered; and now the sneaky bugger was trying to catch me out, wanting to know if I had any guilty secrets to reveal. I couldn't be fooled that easily.

'The only reason I can think of Sir,' I replied, 'is that you want to formally welcome me to your Division, and you couldn't do it last week because I was working nights.' Good answer Dave, I secretly said to myself. A smart move to mention the night shift, this bloke probably hadn't worked after dark for years, if ever, office hours were more his cup of tea.

'No, that is not why you are here,' he snapped, obviously not appreciating my flippant answer. His response confirmed my suspicion, he was a man who didn't work when the sun went down and the bad lads came out to play.

'You are here because there's been an official complaint about you.' He let that remark hang in the air whilst my mind was busy working overtime. Bloody hell, I thought, what on earth could that be about, I've only been here for a week and he's telling me that someone has already complained about me! I remained silent. Don't give him any bullets to fire at you Dave, I told myself.

'Don't you want to know what the complaint's about?' he asked impatiently.

'Yes Sir, don't think I've done anything wrong though,' I answered, rather lamely.

He exhaled noisily, shook his head slightly as though he was speaking to the village idiot. 'You crashed a panda car in Elland last year,' he finally told me.

At last I had the answer, I breathed a little easier, oh is that all it is, thank goodness for that I thought. I remembered the incident clearly enough, and that particular bump had been something and nothing, but this sneaky bugger was suggesting that I was in some sort of serious trouble.

'Oh yes Sir,' I replied, trying to disguise my obvious relief. 'That was six months ago and I thought it had been finalised.'

'Hmm, it would appear that it was your third crash in the last five years. And that means that it was automatically referred to the Discipline and Complaints Department [D & C] for investigation.'

That didn't sound quite right to me, I shook my head slightly before answering. 'Don't think it was the third one Sir.'

He looked back down at his desk. He had my personal record laid out before him, he flicked through the paperwork before quoting the dates and locations of the other two incidents. Sounded much worse than it really was, but armed with that information I was now able to stand my corner.

'The first one you mentioned Sir, was a stolen car, its driver deliberately rammed me during a car chase; and the second incident wasn't even a crash. It was just that the tyres were slashed on my panda car when it was parked up in a rough part of town. At the time I was inside a house taking a burglary report so I didn't think that it should even be classed as a crash. I admit that the last one was my fault but that was the only blameworthy crash as far as I'm concerned.'

There was an awkward silence as he digested my explanation. Then, having finished that little speech in my defence, I was left to reflect that maybe I'd been a bit too argumentative, especially when this was the first time that I'd met the bloke. He wasn't finished with me yet, he had a job to do and right now that job was to admonish me.

'Well, PC Watson, the bottom-line is that there have been three occasions in the last five years when the police car which you were responsible for was damaged,' he stated. No arguing with that, no matter how unfair it may be.

'Yes Sir,' was my feeble response.

Maybe now he felt a little sorry for me. 'Don't look so worried PC Watson, the good news is that D & C don't intend to take any further action against you. They have left it to my discretion to deal with you as I think fit.' He waited for an answer, but when he didn't get one he continued speaking anyway.

'I have decided that there will be an entry logged in the Divisional Register confirming that I have advised you about your driving.'

'Yes Sir, thank you Sir,' I grudgingly replied, although I didn't really think that I had anything to thank him for.

'And one more thing before you leave PC Watson, don't crash any of my cars, or I'll have your driving permit taken away. Do remember, you're no good to me without a permit.'

I stood up and came to attention, replaced my helmet firmly on my head and remembered to salute again before turning to leave. Then back down the stairs to the control room where they were waiting for my return.

'Well then Dave, have you been sacked?' asked Inspector Holden.

'No boss, just a rollocking, and an entry in the Divisional Register, whatever that is supposed to be. I've never even heard of such a register before.' He gave me a puzzled look, obviously expecting a more detailed explanation. 'It's because I crashed a panda car in Elland last year.'

'Oh that's all right then,' he replied, smiling at me now. 'For a minute there I thought it was something serious.'

I left the office and returned to my panda car, there were jobs still to be done that had been reported hours ago.

A burglary to attend, then a couple of cars that had been screwed. Later on it might be a car crash to deal with or a someone missing from home or a report of a sudden death or an industrial accident. The possibilities were endless. Manningham was a busy place to work, no wonder the Super was so concerned about me losing my driving permit.

Despite my first introduction to the Superintendent I soon settled in and felt completely at home working in Bradford. It was the city of my birth, I was born not half a mile away from the police station where I now worked. The Manningham district is one of the most deprived areas of Bradford but for me it had a familiarity about it. My parents had both grown up there, they went to school there and after they married they had their first home there. I soon realised that although I was new to the Division I was also one of the most experienced officers on the team. And that meant that I was expected to continue in my role as a tutor constable for recruits.

Within a few weeks I was introduced to my next proba-tioner, Peter Baker. He was a good bloke and a bit older than the typical recruit. Peter would be under my guidance for the next ten weeks of his training.

Back in those days Bradford had a number of police stations scattered around the inner city and its suburbs. Suspects arrested from within the city boundary were usually taken to the central custody area which was known as 'The Bridewell', an impressive sounding place but in reality little more than a modern concrete dungeon in the basement of Bradford Central Police Station. The high incidents of crime in Manningham meant that we were making arrests almost every day with regular trips to the Bridewell. I soon realised that it had a character all of its own; the constant noise from screaming and shouting prisoners made it an intimidating place, voices echoing around the concrete walls. Anyone walking through that heavy steel entrance door for the first time would be taken aback by a smell which is unique to that building. It's probably the smell of unwashed bodies, together with the stench of vomit and urine from the many drunks who are frequently incarcerated within those cells.

The man in charge of this hellhole is the custody sergeant; and he usually rules his domain with an iron fist. Answerable to no-one, it is he who decides if a suspect will be detained or released; or if the suspect is eventually charged, the custody sergeant will determine who will be released on bail and who will be detained in the cells. In short, the custody sergeant's word was law in the Bridewell and he is a man who demanded respect.

On one particular night I was working with Peter when we started to follow a clapped out old banger being driven by a boy racer. Within minutes this 'follow' became a high-speed car chase through the streets of inner-city Bradford. A radio call to Control soon confirmed that it was a stolen car. The chase followed a familiar pattern, the car was being driven far too fast for the conditions, the driver failed to negotiate a tight bend before skidding across the road and coming to a grinding halt when it finally crashed into a lamp post. The driver's door was instantly thrown open and the thief was out of the car and sprinting away down the road. Likewise, we were after him and catching up quickly. After a short foot chase we caught and arrested the lad and we were soon heading for the cells at the Bridewell. All routine stuff really, so much so that I expected that within a couple of hours we would be back on the streets looking for our next customer.

But first we faced the dubious pleasure of the Bridewell. On some nights it would be so busy that it could take hours just to get your prisoner into a cell and complete the initial paperwork. On other nights it would be less busy but you may still face a custody sergeant who was deliberately being obstructive and making life difficult for the arresting officers.

Tonight we were in luck, the waiting room was deserted, which was always a good sign. In we went, told our prisoner to sit on the bench and wait for our turn. It's at this point that many prisoners engage the arresting officers in conversation, probably because there's nothing else to do. The more vocal ones will share a joke or pass-on the local gossip. More often they'll ask their arresting officers what happens next, especially if they haven't been arrested before. Understandably they'll want to know when they will be released, or charged, or remanded in custody. But that wasn't the case tonight, our man simply looked down at the floor, obviously sulking about his arrest and refusing to speak.

The booming shout of 'NEXT!' confirmed that it was now our turn to introduce our prisoner to the custody sergeant. I expected that he would be stood behind his desk and alongside him should be his sidekick, typically a constable whose job was to help with the paperwork. I pushed open the heavy inter-connecting door and we walked through. The custody desk was directly in front of us, and there stood Sergeant Welsh. But this time he appeared to be alone. The room is barely ten foot square but a quick look round confirmed that Sergeant Welsh was indeed alone. He stood looking at us, his ginger moustache twitching as he waited to hear the circumstances of the arrest. I had known this particular custody sergeant for some time and knew that he was blessed with a dry, and sometimes, a wicked sense of humour.

I thought no more about the absence of his sidekick and instead went directly into my spiel, told him about the car chase and the arrest of the sulky youth now stood alongside me. Then it was the sergeant's turn to speak to our suspect about his arrest. Some prisoners often take this opportunity to deny the account given by the arresting officer, others demand their right to have a solicitor informed of their arrest. But not our prisoner, he was still giving us the silent treatment and refusing to speak. Instead he continued to stare miserably down at the floor.

The silence dragged on. I was puzzled by this unexpected delay until something happened which nearly made me jump back with fright. From behind my left shoulder I had a fleeting glimpse of a fluorescent green object emerge from behind the desk with startling speed. As the object darted skywards I whipped my head round to see a glove puppet of Kermit the Frog not six inches from my left ear, and when the bloody thing first shot up into the air it set my heart racing. Until that moment I'd been stood with my left elbow leaning casually on the desk, that was until Kermit's sudden appearance nearly gave me heart failure. Now for the first time our prisoner looked up wide-eyed and stared straight ahead. The poor lad was like a rabbit caught in a car's head-lights. Kermit had certainly grabbed his attention. We all watched as its head twitched from side to side in quick jerky movements before peering directly into the face of our shocked prisoner.

Peter and I were now in stitches, watching the puppet's mouth open and close in perfect unison with the voice which emerged from somewhere below the desk. I recognised that voice, it belonged to Sergeant Welsh's missing sidekick, and this repertoire had obviously been well practiced. Right now it was being performed to perfection. Kermit's head suddenly darted forward, the long green neck stretching out over the desk until it was only inches away from our shocked prisoner. Then, as its mouth opened and closed, it started asking questions.

'Right kid, what's your name?'

Our prisoner remained silent, didn't want to play this silly little game no matter how funny we happened to think it was. Kermit however was determined to have answers, he leaned a little further forward, the huge mouth now almost touching the nose of our prisoner.

'You heard me kid.' The thief looked up and faced Kermit. 'Yes I'm talking to you kid,' shouted Kermit. 'I asked you what's your name.'

Although Peter and I thought the whole situation was hilarious our prisoner didn't find things quite so amusing. He quickly backed away from Kermit and after the initial shock he was now sulking again. Remaining resolutely silent he refused to talk to Kermit or answer the questions. There was a pause, only broken by the sniggering coming from me and Peter. So far Sergeant Welsh hadn't shown the slightest flicker of a smile but we'd reached stalemate and somehow this process had to be moved forward. Kermit was certainly providing some light hearted entertainment but we weren't going to get this lad's details until he decided to speak. Time for a change of plan.

'Look son, you heard what Kermit asked you, so answer the question and tell us your bloody name?' demanded Sergeant Welsh.

There was now anger in his voice, a suggestion of impatience and a little more pressure applied to our prisoner. At the same time Kermit's head swivelled constantly backwards and forwards, looking first at Sergeant Welsh and then back to the prisoner waiting for an answer.

The added pressure from Sergeant Welsh soon had the desired result. Our prisoner's resolve had cracked and he was now willing to speak; and unbelievably he gave his answer directly to Kermit. At last something of a breakthrough, the new rules of the game were firmly established. We then went through the whole 'booking in' process, with Kermit asking the questions, reluctantly answered by our prisoner and then written down by Sergeant Welsh. It was perfect synchronization, each of them speaking in turn; first the questions from Kermit, then the answer from our sulking prisoner, and finally Sergeant Welsh would complete the paperwork. 'Thank you gentleman,' he added, 'move on to the next question if you please Kermit.' It took Kermit only a few more minutes to obtain the lad's name and address and his date of birth. Then it was his occupation and finally his medical history, in fact everything we needed, other than a full confession to the crime.

When Kermit finished questioning the prisoner he turned his attention to me.

'Right Officer, that's all done, take him away now and put him in a cell.'

Was I really being told what to do by a bloody glove puppet? Sergeant Welsh looked on impassively as though this pantomime was just an everyday occurrence at the Bridewell. We left the custody desk and walked through into the cell corridor to find the next vacant cell. For the first time in almost an hour the prisoner spoke directly to me.

'They were just taking the piss in there, I knew what it was, I'm not stupid you know, I knew that it was someone's arm inside that Kermit.'

Well this lad's quick isn't he? He was right of course and they had probably played the same trick on every prisoner for the last few hours.

Soon it was time to leave the Bridewell, we would return later to interview our prisoner. As we made our way out of the building I again heard the now familiar voice of Kermit shouting, 'NEXT!' Doubtless the incoming prisoner was about to have the same reception. They can be long, and sometimes boring nights in the Bridewell and I suppose that officers who work there had to entertain themselves somehow.

Working at Bradford would be very different from Brighouse, but for me it felt like I had come home. It had been a difficult decision to leave Brighouse after seven years. At times I felt as though I was starting again but I was sure that I'd made the right decision and for the time being I was enjoying life.

Here I am as young police recruit. (*DW*)

Looking smart, as PC 1021
David Watson, wearing a
police helmet. (*DW*)

A sample of my police items and emblems. (*DW*)

Brighouse, my first patch/foot beat. (*DW*)

The open market at Brighouse, the scene of 'Daylight Robbery' (Chapter 1). (*DW*)

Police and pickets clash during the 1984/85 miners' strike. (*Courtesy of the late Arthur Wakefield / Brian Elliott collection*)

King Street, Brighouse, where I nearly became a midwife, the situation described in 'Merry Christmas' (Chapter 3). (*DW*)

Years ago, this building was the scene of the 'brothel-raid', described in 'Carry on Capers' (Chapter 7). (*DW*)

The rather uninspiring exterior of Brighouse police station. (*DW*)

Entrance to Bingley police station and the stone steps described in 'Leading by Example' (Chapter 15). (*DW*)

Dalton Lane, Keighley, the place where the car chase ended in 'Crazy Pursuit' (Chapter 14). (*DW*)

Worth Valley Police and Community Control point, Haworth, where Mrs Crawford called after her car had been clamped, as described in 'Clampers' (Chapter 16). (*DW*)

The notorious Pay & Display at the Changegate Car Park in Haworth, where clamping was rigidly enforced (Chapter 16). (*DW*)

The tourist hot spot of Haworth, featured in 'Clampers' (Chapter 16). (*DW*)

Looking smart, as PC 1021 David Watson, wearing a traffic police cap. (*DW*)

CHAPTER 9

Testing Times

I felt helpless, completely useless. Within minutes of arriving at this job I knew that I was out of my depth, not a feeling which I enjoyed. I'd been a copper for over eight years and was one of the most experienced blokes on the shift but right now I didn't have a clue what to do next. Yes I was from the emergency services, and I was here in my official capacity at the request of a woman whose name I had already forgotten. Her name was Claire, and for her I was obviously from the wrong branch of the emergency services, but that didn't matter. Nor did it lower my own feeling of guilt about being unable to provide any real help for Claire or her husband.

Harry was sixty-four years old, a heavy goods driver with only eleven months to work before his retirement. He looked remarkably fit, tall and slim with no sign of the paunch normally associated with truck drivers. Claire was his wife of over forty years but right now she was crying and pleading with him, begging him to listen to what this policeman was saying. Her words weren't having any effect. Harry was in a world of his own, and it wasn't a world that I ever want to experience.

I had been in their home for less than ten minutes but already it felt like hours. I was at a house in Kings Road in Bradford, a pleasant residential area in the city's suburbs, not the sort of place where I anticipated problems when the message first came over the radio.

'Alpha Charlie 2,' called our radio op. 'Go ahead,' I replied, then came the rest of the message. 'Can you attend at the following address ...' He passed the details over the air before saying, 'The ambulance and a doctor are already on their way so they should be there to meet you.'

'Yes okay, show me attending, but what's actually happening there?'

'Alpha Charlie 2, we don't know for certain, sounds like an elderly man is having something of a mental breakdown. It's his wife that phoned, she says he's seriously ill and threatening to smash up the house.'

That was the full extent of the information. Within minutes I was pulling up outside the house. No sign of an ambulance or the doctor's car but my first impressions were encouraging enough. For a start it was quiet, nothing to suggest that a disturbance was taking place. I left the car and walked along the garden path. Couldn't help but admire the beautiful garden, everything neat and tidy, the sort of place where someone takes pride in their horticultural skills.

At the front door I had a quick look round. Still nothing to suggest that there was anything amiss. Then, just as I was about to knock, the large picture window to my left suddenly exploded into a million pieces. Bloody hell! I wasn't expecting that. I leapt out of the way as a television was hurled through the window from inside the house. I looked down to where it landed and watched it roll end over end before coming to a stop. The back panel had become detached and the screen shattered, leaving glass fragments glistening on the lawn. Then I heard the sound of a woman's voice, not young, not particularly old either, but it was a desperate and pleading voice.

'Harry, no, no, please Harry stop it, stop it please.'

Looked like Harry was practising his shot-putt technique by hurling a 26-inch TV straight through the window, and this was just the start. This wasn't the time to knock on the door and wait patiently for it to be opened. I now knew the urgency of the job and I needed to be inside this house, not stood waiting at the door. I tried the door handle, damn, it was locked. I banged hard on the door with the flat of my palm, loud urgent banging as I shouted, 'It's the police, come and open the door.' I kept banging and shouted again. Then the same woman's voice.

'Harry the police are here to help you, please Harry sit down till I let them in.'

A moment later I heard a key turn in the lock and the door was pulled open. Claire stood facing me, tears rolling down her cheeks, fear in her eyes.

'It's Harry.' That was the only thing she said, it was all she needed to say. I walked quickly past her and through into the dining room where Harry was now sat in the dark. I fumbled for the light switch, located it and flicked the switch. For the first time I saw him properly. His craggy features and his strong square jaw gave the impression that he was a physically tough man, but sadly he was now also a broken man. I called out his name but he didn't move. He remained sat on a dining chair with his back to me, both arms stretched out in front of him and his head resting on the table. Claire followed me into the room and stood alongside her husband, probably feeling the need to explain his behaviour.

'Oh I'm so sorry officer,' she said, 'but we've just had some terrible news, Harry's been back to the hospital today ... they told us the results of his tests.'

I turned to face her, not quite knowing what to say, didn't want to make her feel any worse than she already did, so all I could do was tell her that everything would be okay and that a doctor would soon be here. I stood and looked at her, wanted to hold her hands and comfort her but at the same time knowing that it wouldn't be the right thing to do. Maybe she felt the need to break the awkward silence, she was crying and trying to talk at the same time, searching for the right words to make sense of this awful situation.

'They've told us ... they said that he's only got a few months left,' she whispered.

Claire never mentioned the word cancer but I'm sure that's what she was talking about. I didn't want to ask, it was almost as though the very word was banned in this household.

Harry hadn't uttered a single word since I entered the house. The silence dragged on as I tried to decide what to do next. I watched as Harry lifted his head off the table and stared directly ahead, he didn't move for several seconds, then he drew his head back and started head-butting the table. Each time his forehead crashed down onto the table it was with greater force than the previous time. There were three, maybe four heavy blows before I had chance to react. I had to stop this somehow, and quickly. I stepped behind him, pulled his head away from the table, interlocking my fingers around his forehead. Harry was now snarling like a wounded animal as both Claire and myself tried to calm him down. He was a strong man and for half a minute we struggled against each other, the sinews in his neck taking the strain, standing out as he twisted and writhed and tried to wrench his head from my grip.

It was like we were in a slow motion wrestling match with a new set of rules, neither one of us being prepared to hurt the other. I was trying to stop Harry from head-butting the table and I think he understood that, at the same time he made no attempt to harm me. Claire stood alongside us, pleading with her husband to stop, cupping his face in her hands like a mother would a child who had fallen over and grazed his knees. I remained behind him, struggling to keep control, silently praying for the arrival of the ambulance and paramedics. I needed to contact Control and ask for assistance but couldn't risk releasing Harry to grab my radio.

Then a spark of intuition from Claire. 'Harry would you like a drink?' she asked. It was a question asked out of desperation. He didn't reply but she walked out of the room anyway and left us to our struggle. She returned a minute later with a tumbler half full of what appeared to be whisky.

'Harry, here drink this,' she instructed as she handed him the glass. The sight of the booze had the desired effect, he stopped struggling, allowing me to release my grip on his forehead. He sat upright and gently took the tumbler from his wife. For a moment he sat motionless staring into the glass. I was unsure about giving him alcohol when he would probably be on medication very soon. But then again, should a dying man be refused his favourite tipple?

Slowly he lifted the glass to his lips before pouring the whole lot down in one go. What now? Would this calm him down or would it make him even more depressed or worse, would he become violent? He set the empty glass down on the table and slowly got to his feet, didn't seem to notice that I was there. When he walked into the hallway I stayed close to him, trying to engage him in conversation but he wasn't having it. He simply ignored my questions and attempts to reassure him that a doctor was on his way. To this poor bloke I was invisible and he completely disregarded anything I said or did. Halfway along the hall he stopped walking and turned to his right where he put the palms of his hands on the wall above his head. For a moment he just stood there before starting to bang the palms of his hands against the wall. Then the wailing started. Harry started repeating the same word over and over: 'No, No, No, No.' They were his first words since I entered the house, it was the cry of a desperate and frightened man and I didn't know how to help him.

I could have guessed what would come next? It was back to the head-butting, only now it was on to a solid brick wall rather than a dining table. Somehow I had to stop him hurting himself, it's drilled into coppers early in their careers that their most important duty is the protection of life, and right now I was failing miserably. I stepped forward and this time I wrapped my arms tightly around his waist and threw myself backwards. I was trying to drag Harry with me and get him away from the wall. He pulled against me with all his strength and together we stumbled about the hallway trying to keep our footing, both of us pulling in opposite directions. But this meant that Harry's arms were free whilst mine were still wrapped tightly around his waist. We bounced from one wall to the other until I saw him reach down and push his left hand inside the shade of a table lamp. It was a deliberate and calculated movement. I tried to pull him away but it was too late, Harry had already wrapped his fingers around the light bulb. It seemed to be happening in slow motion but still I couldn't stop him. The bulb had to be very hot, it had been switched on since I first entered the house but he never flinched. Again I pulled him backwards with all the force that I could muster. We both stumbled, which caused the lamp to fall over but Harry held onto the bulb. I yelled at him to let go, Claire was also pleading with him but it was like he was in a trance and couldn't hear us. Instead he squeezed his fingers tightly around the bulb and crushed it with his bare hand.

The hallway was suddenly thrown into darkness. Only the ceiling light from the dining room now providing any light. I doubled my efforts and yanked him backwards, throwing him on to the floor before falling down on top of him. Fragments of the hot broken light bulb were in his clenched fist and I watched with horror as he laid face down onto the floor and shoved the remaining shards of glass into his mouth. The poor man was trying to eat what was left of the light bulb. To actually witness someone having a mental breakdown right before your eyes is a very frightening experience, not something which I had ever come across before.

But how could I stop Harry hurting himself, and do so without using too much force to restrain him? The last thing I wanted was to risk injuring a man who I was supposed to be helping. He was an elderly man, if I grabbed him too hard or held him down too forcefully then I would certainly bruise his skin, and possibly even break his wrists. I couldn't even use the normal restraints such as arm locks or handcuffs. Harry wasn't a violent prisoner. I was used to dealing with such people but this was very different, he was a sick man whose mind was disturbed and he wanted to hurt himself. Our wrestling match continued as we grappled with each other and rolled around on the floor. I tried desperately to pull his hands away from his face but realised that I was too late on hearing his teeth crunch the broken glass. I cursed myself for reacting so slowly. Even in the gloom of the darkened hallway I could see a trickle of blood seep out from between his lips. He continued to chew the broken glass but there was nothing I could do to stop him from swallowing it.

Then there was a knock on the door and a loud and confident shout.

'Hello, it's the doctor.'

A middle-aged Asian gentleman stepped inside, he saw us on the floor and despite the gloom he instantly understood what was happening. Between sobs Claire explained the problem about her husband. We were all squashed into the narrow hallway, Harry face down on the floor with me laid on top of him, trying to hold him down with his arms stretched out above his head and out of harms way. The doctor crouched down alongside us and made his assessment, Claire was alongside me, gently stroking Harry's hair. Much to my relief the doctor decided to give Harry an injected tranquilizer, it would calm him down and then he could be taken to hospital.

Within minutes of the injection Harry had stopped struggling, the tranquilizer was working its magic allowing me to release him. The ambulance crew had also arrived and they strapped a now much subdued Harry onto the stretcher. We were all mightily relieved when they carried him from the house and into the back of the waiting ambulance. Claire would accompany him to hospital. Only after they left could I collect my thoughts and arrange for the broken window to be boarded up before going on to the next job. After this experience I hoped that the rest of the night would be a little less stressful. Maybe I'd get something which was relatively straightforward, such as a drunken pub fight or a high-speed car chase, perhaps I'd catch a burglar in the act or deal with a violent domestic, surely anything would be better than this.

CHAPTER 10

Into Battle

There was a feeling of nostalgia when leaving Bradford's Queens Road nick for the last time. This dilapidated old building had been the home to generations of coppers but was now well past its sell-by-date. For me it had been a great place to work, and I was not looking forward to leaving.

So the Manningham Division and its colourful history were to disappear forever. Our new station, some two miles away, would be renamed as Eccleshill Division. Surprisingly it wasn't even in the district of Eccleshill. It was actually in the neighbouring district of Idle, but the Chief Constable didn't want to call our prestigious new nick by its more accurate name of 'Idle Police Station'. No, that would be far too embarrassing. So to solve this problem the long standing boundary between the two districts was manipulated and our new nick was officially now in Eccleshill. We were moving, lock stock and barrel, to a brand new building, a purpose-built police headquarters.

The new building was very different from the old one. It was spacious, clean and tidy rather than cramped and cluttered and smelly. There was a huge car park, a fully-staffed canteen and even a spacious licensed bar. Then there was the gymnasium, numerous storerooms and our own prisoner cell block. It wasn't long before Eccleshill was seen as a desirable place to work, something that seldom happened at the old place, but now officers from surrounding Divisions were submitting transfer requests to join us. The result was that we had more coppers on each team, there were more specialized departments and more senior officers. All of a sudden our new bigger, brighter division seemed to have everything going for it, everything that is, apart from a sense of belonging, and the feeling that we were no longer part of a close-knit team.

New bosses were brought in to try and re-create the old team spirit. Both the sergeant and inspector on my team were recent additions. Eccleshill was a new challenge for them, a place where they were determined to make a name for themselves.

So we were now based in a more affluent suburb but we still had responsibility for many of the deprived areas. That meant that our main source of work still came from either the many council estates we policed or from inner city areas. The most notorious of those estates was Ravenscliffe. To the casual observer Ravenscliffe is no different from the others but it's plagued by a frighteningly high crime rate, a place where young lads rarely attended school and older teenagers had little chance of finding employment. They would often spend their teenage years living off benefits just like their parents had done before them.

House burglaries and car thefts were daily events. Joy-riders in stolen cars had little to fear from the police. They would tear around the streets at breakneck speed and think nothing of skidding around corners, bouncing up pavements or practising their 'doughnuts' and 'handbrake turns' on the public roads, often within yards of younger kids playing in the street. Eventually one of the more law abiding residents would find the courage to phone the police, and even that was usually done anonymously to avoid retribution.

It was a 'lawless society', and close to being a no-go area for the police. So I listened with interest one evening when a radio message directed Steve on to the estate. He was driving a panda car, crewed up with Linda, and going to a report of a bonfire party. The street they were heading for had a bad reputation. Steve was expecting trouble. Daylight was already fading but Steve was wise enough not to drive the panda car straight into the cul-de-sac, that would be just inviting trouble.

From a safe distance they saw the bonfire, piled high with broken furniture, a settee, a dining table and a double bed amongst other things. A crowd had gathered to enjoy the spectacle and were treating the bonfire as a social occasion. For some it was an evening out, a bonfire night party that had come three weeks early. A ghetto-blaster played punk rock at full volume. There was dancing around the garden, others stood and swigged beer straight from the bottle. Sausages and burgers were on the menu, the fire being used as a makeshift barbecue so that everyone could have a jolly old time.

Steve and Linda walked cautiously towards the fire but were soon met with abuse and obscenities. A volley of bricks and bottles followed, all falling short, but a powerful message all the same. These partygoers didn't want coppers spoiling their night, so my colleagues wisely beat a tactful retreat and drove down the road to relative safety. Only then did Steve radio through to Control; things were getting out of hand, he reported, potential for serious disorder. They were instructed to withdraw from the area and return to the police station to see the inspector.

Des Morley was our inspector, he wanted to know what had happened. On hearing Steve's explanation our new boss was in his element. He was recently posted to Eccleshill from the Task Force, a department with particular skills in dealing with large-scale public disorder. The scene that Steve described was like music to his ears.

A radio message was now passed over the air. Every officer in the division was ordered to return to the police station immediately to see Inspector Morley. My ears pricked up! That sort of instruction was most unusual. I couldn't imagine why he needed to see the whole shift at once, so it had to be something serious. Twenty minutes later we all assembled in the briefing room where Steve brought us up to date. Inspector Morley then took over and told us about a recent phone call to our control room.

'A man called Richard Clarke phoned about five minutes ago. He was supposed to be the new tenant of 21 Marshfield Close and only picked up the keys to his new house yesterday.

Apparently he's already moved some of his furniture into the house, but he wasn't going to move the rest of his stuff in until next week. However, it looks like his new neighbours have forced his door and nicked all his belongings, it's his stuff that's now on the bonfire. As we've just heard, Steve and Linda interrupted the celebrations and the natives didn't like it. Well, we're not going to let these people get away with it, so Sergeant North will now explain how we will deal with the situation.'

Inspector Morley sat down and left Sergeant Adam North to take centre stage; he was a man known to be capable of sudden and unexpected aggression, with a reputation which preceded him on his arrival at our Division.

'Right this is the plan,' he announced. 'We'll be taking two vans down there, eight of you in each van.' He turned to me and a colleague and said, 'Dave you'll be driving the first van, and Simon you'll be driving the second one. We go in with grills over the windscreens in case we get bricked. I want no pussyfooting around, it's straight onto their street and then everyone out of the vans – and be quick about it. Get over the fence and into the garden. We aim to arrest the whole lot of them, right ... any questions?'

'What about the females?' asked Linda.

'Arrest all the blokes first, then if there's any room left in the vans fill them up with the women.'

'What are we arresting them for?' asked someone from behind.

'Burglary for a start, they've broken into that bloke's house and nicked his furniture, and if we can't prove that, then we'll go for arson instead.'

It was an outspoken and blunt briefing, leaving us in no doubt about what was expected. This wasn't going to be a typical criminal investigation, it was a raiding party to exact some form of retribution. Our objective was clear: we were going into a hostile situation, and the priority was to take prisoners; and we'd only worry about a criminal investigation after the arrests had been made. Five minutes later both vans were pulling away from the station. We drove the three miles to Ravenscliffe in convoy. Sergeant North sat alongside me and gave me my instructions.

'Right Dave, drive straight in, get in there fast and stop right at the side of the bonfire.' He then turned round and spoke to our colleagues behind us. 'Listen in lads,' he barked, the excited chatter suddenly stopped, he had their attention now, 'I want everyone out of that door and over the garden fence before this bloody van even stops moving, and don't come back without a prisoner each; is that understood?'

'Yes boss,' was the collective reply.

The second van was close behind as I turned left off Ravenscliffe Avenue. Then it was left again before a sharp right into Marshfield Close. We entered the cul-de-sac, barely a hundred yards long, and for the first time I saw the blazing bonfire. The second van was now so close behind that it was almost touching my rear bumper, and we were travelling at quite a speed for such a short road. At the same time I heard the lads in the back of our van pulling open the sliding side door, everyone ready for a quick exit. Within seconds I was alongside the bonfire, I bounced the van up onto the nearside footpath and at the same time hit the brakes. We skidded to a stop, not ten feet from the flames but already we were being pelted by beer bottles. One bottle bounced off the wire grill covering the windscreen, another bounced off the van roof. Sergeant North was already out of the van and hurdling the garden fence, an intimidating sight when charging into the middle of a hostile crowd. The flames reflected off his bald head and for a split second he was the very image of a screaming Sioux warrior charging into battle, lacking only war paint on his face and a tomahawk in his right hand.

As I removed the ignition keys the rest of the lads were out of the van and following Sergeant North into battle. A quick glance in my rear view mirror confirmed that the occupants of the second van were doing exactly the same, it was a complete melee. There was chaos everywhere, music still belting out from the ghetto-blaster, punches being thrown, a beer bottle in the wrong hands became a makeshift cosh.

There was shouting and screaming everywhere, people diving over garden fences to escape, others standing and fighting, arms and legs flaying in every direction. Men were being thrown to the ground, arms twisted up backs and hand-cuffs slapped on wrists. Those already locked-up were being dragged back over the garden fence, many of them carried horizontally and launched into the back of the vans. The music suddenly stopped when the system was accidentally kicked into the flames. This wasn't a planned arrest for any specific offence, it was more like a mass brawl, a good old fashioned street fight between two opposing gangs, but thankfully the good guys were winning! Amongst all the screaming and shouting there was one voice which was louder than all the others, it was a familiar voice and was delivering what could only be described as a war cry.

'Come on lads, fuck 'em, fuck 'em all, every one of 'em.'

It was the unmistakable voice of our Sergeant, I'm sure that his shouted command was just a rallying call to his troops rather than a specific instruction. Well, at least I hoped it was.

In less than three minutes both vans were full to bursting. Prisoners squashed into the small cage at the back and colleagues returned to their seats in the middle section of the van. Some officers were now rather dishevelled whilst others sported the odd bruise or graze. The bonfire still burned fiercely but the gardens were now deserted apart from a couple of women who continued to shout abuse as I reversed out of the narrow street. Two heavily laden vans chugged back up the hill to the police station ready to discharge their human cargo. Back at the nick fifteen prisoners climbed out of the two vans to trudge into the cell block. They too showed signs of having being in a battle, and now they would be spending the rest of the night in our cells.

There was an upbeat mood in the cell area. I heard colleagues comparing stories and injuries, tales being told about falling over the garden fence, others recalled ducking out of the way of a punch or a beer bottle. Tales were repeated about which prisoner they had arrested or the identity of the those who may have escaped; there was a real sense of camaraderie and a feeling of shared danger. A new team spirit was starting to emerge, one which had been lacking before this incident.

The criminal investigation could now begin. It resulted in only two of the prisoners being charged with breaking into the neighbour's house and setting fire to his furniture. The other thirteen were eventually released without charge. But they'd all have a story to tell, one that would sound so far fetched that few people would believe it to be true.

I suppose some people may consider that the police response in this case had been too extreme, maybe it was too violent. A throwback to yesteryear when the police didn't worry about being politically correct. Perhaps tonight's incident was from a time when Britain still had a 'Police Force' that was feared by criminals rather than today's 'Police Service' which panders to the whim of politicians.

And my opinion on the matter? Well for what it's worth, this happened nearly twenty years ago, before media scrutiny and mass access to mobile phones and their built-in cameras. Few people saw what really happened on that night, and even fewer took any notice. But I was sure that Inspector Dirk Morley and Sergeant Adam North were the right people, working in the right place at the right time, and most importantly, they got the right result.

CHAPTER 11

That Wise Old Cat

I read the notice again: 'Community Constable wanted at Bingley'. Now that would make a pleasant change, I thought. Quite unexpectedly the prospect of walking a foot beat again was rather appealing, especially in a pleasant little town like Bingley. Had to be better than dashing around in a panda car with little time to investigate jobs properly. The more I thought about such a move the more inviting it became. Another bonus was that I drove through Bingley every day on my way to Bradford so the location would be perfect too. Within the hour I had applied for the post. A week or so later I was told that my application was successful and I would soon be back to pounding the beat again. For the first time in years I started to adapt to a much slower pace of life.

One afternoon I'd just left the nick when I heard my call sign on the radio. I answered but my next job was to be so unusual that even the radio operator didn't know what to make of it. A pet cat, he told me, had been stolen. That's strange, I thought, I'd never heard of the theft of a cat before, didn't even know that thieves stole cats; pedigree dogs are sometimes stolen, horses too, and cattle, almost certainly, but stolen cats, no, can't say that I'd ever come across that before.

Half an hour later I was outside the house in question, number 48, a 'For Sale' sign fixed to the front wall with a 'SOLD' sign proudly attached. It was a quality house in a pleasant area and not the sort of place where I expected the usual problems. I pushed open the wrought-iron gate and walked towards the front door, rang the bell and waited for an answer. The door was opened by a smartly dressed chap, about seventy years old, I guessed. He smiled warmly as he spoke.

'Ah officer, do come in, I take it you've come about Percy?'

'Erm, I think I've come about a cat,' I replied.

'Oh, yes, sorry,' he said. 'I'm Mr Sullivan, Percy is our cat. Well, at least I think he's still our cat. Please go through to the living room. I'll pop into the kitchen and make some tea, then I'll come through and tell you what's happened. Just step in there and take a seat, I'll join you in a minute.'

I walked through the hallway and into the spacious living room, the plush cream carpet suddenly making me conscious of my heavy police boots. Too late to take them off now. I looked behind and was relieved to see that there was no muddy trail. On looking up from the carpet I saw that I wasn't alone in the room, an elderly woman sat staring out of the window. She glanced across at me, looking awkward and slightly embarrassed by my presence. I noticed that her eyes were reddened and she held a damp handkerchief in her clenched fist.

'I've come about the cat,' I said, not knowing what else to say to the poor woman. She nodded, dabbed her eyes again before gesturing for me to sit down. There was a mood of sadness and despondency about her. I was puzzled, maybe this job was going to be rather more serious than I first thought.

I felt uneasy, not really knowing what to expect or how to start a conversation. The woman remained silent and gently sobbed into her handkerchief. A minute or two later the tension was lifted slightly when her husband walked in, now carrying a silver tray with three delicate china cups and a steaming pot of tea. He sat down alongside me and offered to do the pouring. That done, he explained the reason for his call. In four days time, he told me, they were due to move house. All the arrangements were in place and they would be moving to a bungalow on the outskirts of town to enjoy their retirement. The story was dragging on a little too long for my liking so I tentatively asked, 'What exactly is it that you want me to do? I thought this was something to do with a cat?'

'That's the point I was coming to,' he said. 'Our Percy has been kidnapped by the woman at number 11, and she won't give him back . . . so we would like you to go down there, talk to the people that live there and bring him home.'

Well, this was certainly something different! Whoever heard of a copper rescuing a kidnapped cat? And who'd want to kidnap a cat anyway?

'Erm, exactly what do you mean when you say he's been kidnapped? I thought that cats usually just came and went as they pleased?'

'Yes, that's right, they do,' he told me. 'But apparently our Percy has been visiting that woman's house for years. I understand that she's been feeding him during all that time and unfortunately we didn't know anything about it. She now claims that Percy is her cat and she won't give him back because she knows that we're about to move house. I think she's worried that Percy won't be able to visit her any more so she's keeping him locked in.'

I sat there with a cup of delicious Earl Grey and considered the difficulties ahead. What should I do if this other woman insists that Percy is her cat? How would I prove who is the true owner? Should I just seize the animal, put it in a cattery and let the court decide the rightful owner? That could take months, maybe years if it went to an appeal. No, that wouldn't work, these people want Percy back before they move house, that's why I'm here. Then I had a spark of inspiration, or so I thought.

'Do you have any documentary evidence to prove that you are the true owners?' I asked. He looked at me blankly and shrugged his shoulders.

'Anything like a receipt from when you bought him? Has he been micro-chipped or registered at a vet's? Anything at all that could identify him?'

'No, sorry,' he replied. 'I don't think we have anything like that.'

Then his wife spoke for the first time. 'We've got that photograph,' she said, pointing to a framed photograph of their beloved cat. I shook my head, I didn't think that a court of law would accept a photograph as proof of ownership. I'd hit another dead-end and was quickly running out of ideas.

'Okay, I'll go down there and see what I can do.'

I finished my tea, stood up and headed for the door, telling Mr Sullivan that I would come straight back, hopefully with their cat, but secretly I didn't hold out much hope. In some ways this was a typical job that a community constable was expected to sort out, and right now I'd rather be doing something else. I walked the short distance to Percy's second home, all the way racking my brains for a solution which would satisfy both parties. It was quite clear to me what had happened. The devious Percy was having the best of both worlds wasn't he, and it had been going on for years. He wasn't daft wasn't Percy, getting fed at two different houses and sharing himself between the two families who were now falling out over his ownership. I did wonder who the fools were, and it certainly wasn't Percy.

Two minutes later I was knocking on the door of number 11. There was no answer so I walked around to the back of the house. Then just as I was just about to knock again I looked inside and saw a cat staring straight at me. It was Percy, a magnificent big black tomcat who was happily sat in the sun looking out of the window. Inside the house I saw an elderly couple. They looked up, startled to see a policeman stood in their back garden. I pointed towards the door and mouthed the words, 'Can you come to the door?'

The door was eventually opened. 'Yes officer,' said the elderly gentleman. 'What can I do for you?'

Well that was a good start, he seemed like a reasonable sort of chap, maybe I could sort this mess out amicably after all. 'Hello Sir,' I nodded towards to the cat and then said, 'I've come about Percy.'

A look of confusion spread across his face but he remained silent for a moment. Then he said, 'I think you've come to the wrong house officer, no one called Percy lives here, just me and the wife. Walter and Elizabeth Gray, that's us, there's no-one here called Percy, never has been.'

'It's about the cat, Percy,' I said, trying to be helpful.

He turned round and looked at the cat, satisfied himself that it was still the same cat and then turned back to me. 'Like I said officer, you've got the wrong house, that's our Buddy, his name's not Percy, sorry, looks like you've come to the wrong place.'

This old chap may have the appearance of being a respectful old gent but as I was finding out, appearances can be deceptive, and he knew why I was there. Not least because he'd already had a similar conversation with Mr Sullivan earlier that day. Now that he had a policeman at his door he suddenly changed and became obnoxious, even tried to close the door in my face. I stood my ground and pushed the palm of my hand against the top of the door to hold it open. 'Look, do you mind if I come in? We need to get this sorted out properly.' I was starting to lose a little patience. Then things turned ugly.

'Have you got a warrant?' he snarled.

'No,' I replied. 'I'm just trying to sort out the ownership of a cat, not arrange for a full-scale drugs bust,' I answered.

'Well bugger off then, and don't come back till you've got a warrant.' This time he slammed the door in my face. I stood there fuming, looking at him through the glass as he shouted, 'Buddy is our cat, he came to us as a stray years ago and we've looked after him ever since. If you don't believe me I suggest you do your job properly and ask the neighbours.'

I walked away, silently cursing both this obnoxious old bugger, and my bad luck for being lumbered with this job. Unresolvable. That's what it was, completely unresolvable. Both couples were convinced that they were the true owners of a cat, which was sharing its time between the two of them. How could I possibly hope to sort this? I went over the definition of theft in my head, reminding myself that the law determines that the original owner of any property will retain that ownership despite someone else having it in their possession. So that's clear enough, the Sullivans remain the true owners. But how could I prove that Buddy and Percy are one and the same animal? It would simply be a matter of opinion, and in this case both parties have a different opinion. Legally it was a minefield yet somehow I was expected to resolve the problem. I couldn't think of any way which would satisfy everyone.

I trudged back to the Sullivan's house, rang the bell and waited for Mr Sullivan to answer.

'The wife will be devastated,' he said when I told him about my visit to number 11. 'She loves cats, probably won't even move house now, she'll not leave here without Percy.' I left him to pass on the bad news after giving him my assurance that I would try to solve the problem. But deep down I had real doubts about resolving this job to his satisfaction.

The following day, I was back at the Sullivans. Outside their house I met Catherine from the Cats Protection League, the same woman who I had spent half an hour on the phone with yesterday. She opened the back doors of her small white van and lifted out a padded crate. Then we walked up the garden path and I pushed the doorbell. Mr Sullivan answered and invited us inside, then, just as he did yesterday, he disappeared into the kitchen to make tea for everyone. Catherine and I walked into the living room where Mrs Sullivan was waiting. I found her to be in a very different mood from yesterday. There was now a smile on her face and she looked thrilled by the prospect of seeing the two tiny white kittens which Catherine was holding.

By the time that Mr Sullivan came in with tea and biscuits it looked like poor old Percy was nothing but a distant memory. His wife was now like a happy little schoolgirl, knelt down on the plush carpet on her hands and knees playing with the two kittens. She didn't know it yet but they would be going with her when she moved to her new home. Mr Sullivan handed me a cup of tea and a flick of his head suggested that he wanted to have a private word in the kitchen. I followed him out of the room, leaving the two women playing with the kittens.

'How did you sort this out lad?' he asked.

'Well, I racked my brains all afternoon yesterday but couldn't think of any way to legally force the Grays to hand Percy back to you,' I explained. 'I checked with the neighbours and unfortunately they did confirm that Percy, or maybe I should say Buddy, had been spending his days at the Gray's house for years; and some of them were prepared to say that in court if necessary.'

Mr Sullivan looked at me, slowly nodding his head in understanding. 'So when we thought that Percy was out hunting mice or birds he was really leading a double life.'

'It looks that way to me,' I agreed, 'so when I got back to the nick I phoned the Cats Protection League, and as you can see, Catherine had just the answer.'

'So what will happen to Percy now?' he asked.

'Well I suggest that he stays at number 11, they have made a pretty good job of looking after him, and I suppose whenever he feels like it he will find himself someone else to feed him. Anyway it looks like your wife has adopted two kittens as replacements for Percy.'

Mr Sullivan had a beaming smile on his face, he shook my hand and thanked me for sorting out the problem. I finished my tea, wished him luck with the house move and said goodbye. On my way back to the nick I walked past number 11. Sat looking out of the window was Percy, or was it Buddy, a fine, independent and elegant-looking animal, a cat who didn't really belong to anyone, so who was I to interfere? After all he was quite capable of deciding for himself where he would live.

It seemed that everyone was happy with the outcome, well everyone apart from me. Wandering back through town I started to question my own role as a copper. Had I really been reduced to sorting out a squabble over the ownership of a domestic cat? Because that's what I'd been doing for the last two days. I felt disillusioned with the sedate pace of life on a community beat. Of course there was some job satisfaction, this incident was one such example. And of course there were other benefits too. I reminded myself that I was fortunate to be working in a relatively stress-free environment. It was also convenient for my home and social life, but still it didn't feel right.

There was another consideration too, one which had been bothering me for some time. I thought about my motives for being a copper. Was I simply looking for a cushy number and an easy life? I already had that, but it wasn't enough. I had to admit, if only to myself, that I didn't become a copper purely to provide a public service. Deep down I still yearned for the thrill of the chase, and for me that meant locking up criminals. Here at Bingley there simply wasn't enough excitement. It was many months since I had arrested a criminal who I caught red-handed. And no longer did I have the opportunity to pit my wits against a hardened criminal in a late night interview. Gone was the job satisfaction that I previously felt when a prisoner confessed to his crime, or proved that a hastily offered alibi was false.

I began to wonder if I would ever feel that familiar tension again when giving evidence in the Crown Court for a serious offence. And much to my surprise, I was actually missing the buzz of going to the chaotic Bridewell cells or taking an injured prisoner to the casualty department at Bradford Royal Infirmary on some crazy Saturday night.

There had been times recently, usually when pounding my beat in the middle of the night, that I found myself switching radio channels rather than listening to the lengthy periods of silence on my own division's channel. Instead I listened with envy to the hectic messages that colleagues in Bradford were attending. Compared to the quiet streets of Bingley the prospect of working nights in Bradford definitely held more appeal. It was time for me to take stock and decide what I really wanted from the job. After mulling things over for a while I realized that I wasn't yet ready to grow old as a community constable.

By now I had a little over twelve years in the job, not yet half way to retirement and I considered myself to be a relatively young and enthusiastic copper. My community beat would be really sought after by many of my colleagues, and the way I now felt they were welcome to it. No, that sort of comfort was not for me, well not yet anyway. I was still seeking that adrenalin rush that you get at the sharp end of policing, and that would mean a move away from Bingley. Later that evening I submitted yet another transfer request.

CHAPTER 12

Marital Bliss

Ten months of being a community constable at Bingley were enough for me. It had been a lovely place to work but it was just too quiet. Probably the right sort of place for the last few years before retirement, but I worried that I was losing touch with the daily cut and thrust of working at a busy division. So I asked for a move, hoping to go back to Bradford, but that was not going to happen. Instead I was transferred just three miles down the valley to the town of Shipley. The divisional boundaries had recently changed and Shipley was now part of the new Bradford North Division, so as far as the management were concerned I had my wish.

That transfer to Shipley had been my fourth move since becoming a copper. It followed periods at Brighouse, then Manningham and Eccleshill in Bradford, and lastly Bingley. Now I was back to my old role of driving a panda car and going to immediate response messages. From now on I was back responding to 999 calls, even though they were not always the sort of jobs one would choose to attend.

Everyone knows that families can fall out with each other, and at times it's a regular event which often follows closing time at pubs and clubs. 'Domestic disputes' is the official police jargon for these incidents, usually abbreviated to 'domestics' and on a Friday or Saturday night that's the one word which every copper dreads hearing over the radio. Tonight it was my turn, my spirits sank when I heard the radio operator's voice.

'Control to Foxtrot Bravo Two, can you go to a domestic in West End Grove, Shipley; we've had a call from the neighbour saying that there's been a hell of a row and it sounds like things are being thrown around the house.'

It was the last thing I wanted to hear. 'Yes, thanks, that's great,' I answered sarcastically. 'Do we know anything about the occupants?'

The control room staff have immediate access to computer records showing domestic disputes going back for years. That sort of information will usually be passed over the radio to the attending officer to warn them about previous incidents.

'Control to Foxtrot Bravo Two,' called Control. 'No, there's no history of domestics at that address.' Well that was a relief anyway, then he sheepishly added, 'But I forgot to tell you that this report came in nearly an hour ago, anonymously. Everyone was busy at the time and unfortunately, you're the first one to come free.'

That really didn't help, but I'd just have to sort it out when I got there. It wouldn't take long, only about a mile to go. Driving through Shipley I thought about the recent changes in police policy when dealing with domestics. A few weeks ago a new instruction came out from headquarters. It required attending officers at domestics to take what the Chief Constable called 'positive action'.

In practice that meant that if there was any evidence of an offence having taken place, such as an assault, or criminal damage, or even something as minor as a breach of the peace, then we were expected to make an arrest. No longer were we allowed to use our own judgement, which in the past often meant that one half of the couple (usually the male) would be taken away in the police car to his friend's or relative's house to sleep off the booze. Then, hopefully by the following day, the reunited couple would make up their differences and play happy families again. Sadly it looked like the days of common sense policing was a thing of the past. We now lived in a world of 'hitting Home Office targets' and that often meant making an arrest just to put a tick in the right box.

I was still mulling this over when I pulled up outside the house in question, thankfully everything appeared to be peaceful. No sound of shouting or screaming, no broken windows or clothing being thrown out of the bedroom windows, definitely so far so good. I informed Control that I'd arrived at the job before locking the car and walking up the garden path to the front door. A loud knock brought no answer. I waited half a minute and knocked again, louder this time, but still no one came. I bent down and pushed open the letter box, put my ear to the door. I could hear a TV but no shouting or screaming, definitely nothing to suggest that a domestic dispute was taking place.

I got back on the radio to Control. 'There's no reply to my knocking and no evidence that a domestic has taken place.' I then asked them to double check that I was at the right address. Yes, came back the reply, this was it, the correct address in West End Grove. So now I had a choice; I could make one last try before I either break down the door to make sure that one of them hadn't murdered the other, or I could assume that it was a malicious call and simply walk away and hope for the best. I tried the door handle, much to my surprise it turned, wasn't locked, so I pushed it open and looked inside, still nothing untoward.

I stepped inside and shouted out, 'Hello, it's the police, is there anybody in?' I was in the home of an elderly couple, the evidence was there to be seen, a dark green lady's coat hung on the bannister, a gent's flat cap on a coat hook; and an umbrella and walking stick were propped up in the corner. Definitely not the home of a young, or even a middle-aged couple. This was becoming more mysterious by the minute, in my experience elderly people don't usually have violent domestics, was I really at the right house?

'Who's that?' came a shouted reply, it was an old man's voice.

'It's the police,' I repeated as I walked through the hallway towards the sound of a TV. I pushed open the lounge door and peered inside. An elderly couple looked at me, both of them well into their seventies. Ernest sat in the chair near the TV, his wife Shirley was sat on the sofa opposite, apart from the sound of the TV they sat in silence. Ernest looked at me, squinted as though he was having trouble focusing his eyes, 'What do you want lad?' he asked.

'We've had a call about a domestic dispute, have you two been falling out?'

'Aye lad, we've had a bit of a row, she's smacked me over me 'ed with me supper.'

Only then did I notice that Ernest's bald head was grazed and now sported an angry looking swelling. The remains of his supper was still on his shirt collar, with bits of carrots and mashed potato smeared on his sleeves and the chair where he sat. On the carpet alongside his chair was what was left of his meal. A black mongrel dog lay in front of the fire and raised its head off the carpet when I walked in. I smiled to myself as the dog wagged its tail and looked pretty content with its lot, having eaten its master's supper off the floor.

'What's your name love?' I asked the woman.

'Shirley, its Shirley Coldwell,' she told me, 'And don't bother checking up on me, you'll not have me on your records, never been in trouble in my life.' Her speech was somewhat slurred, a half empty bottle of brandy lay on the floor at the side of the sofa. It told its own story, she was probably just as drunk as Ernest.

'Have you done this to Ernest?' I asked, pointing at his injured head.

'I 'ave lad,' she proudly announced, 'and ee deserves it, serves 'im right for coming in drunk when pubs shut, 'is supper is ruined, then ee shouts at me and calls me a silly old cow.'

'Aye, cause that's wot you are, nowt but a silly old cow,' chuckled Ernest.

Shirley ignored his interruption and continued, 'And ee walloped me, ee did, ee won't tell you that will ee? Swiped me across me chops, good and proper.'

Oh no, I thought, this really was getting worse by the minute, it wasn't what I wanted to hear, I had hoped to walk away from here after giving a bit of friendly advice and a warning about their future conduct, but it wasn't looking good. I took a deep breath and started going through the motions. 'Did you hit her Ernest?' I asked.

'Aye lad, I did,' he admitted, 'but only after she 'it me wit plate over me 'ed.'

It was hard to believe that this squabble had taken place over an hour ago. They'd had their little dispute but were now back to normal, whatever 'normal' may be in this household. I was sure that there wouldn't be any more trouble tonight, they'd reconciled their differences to a certain extent but my hands were tied by the recent instructions from HQ. They were both telling me that they had assaulted each other, meaning that they would both have to be arrested. It was the sort of job that would previously result in a friendly warning and that would be the end of it, but sadly, not anymore. I scratched my head trying to think of any way round the new directive but, unfortunately, there wasn't one. Everything said over the radio is recorded, including the initial phone call so I had no choice other but to follow the new directive.

'I'm really sorry to tell you this,' I told them, 'but I have to arrest both of you for assault. I wish there was some other way but my hands are tied I'm afraid.'

A mischievous grin now spread across Shirley's face. She seemed quite excited about being arrested. 'Ooh, does that mean we'll go to prison? I've never been arrested before,' she said.

'No Shirley, you won't be going to prison but you might have to sit in a police cell for a couple of hours until you're both sober.'

Ernest didn't share his wife's excitement, 'What about me dog?' he asked.

'Don't worry Ernest, the dog will be all right here by himself, you'll be back home in a few hours.'

Now for the next problem, I had two elderly prisoners who were both drunk. Ideally they should be taken to the cells in separate cars to prevent any further incidents. But Control had just informed me that everyone else was busy, and that meant that I'd have to take them both at the same time. I reached down and switched off the TV, helped Ernest to his feet and saw for the first time that he was a bit wobbly. The booze, followed by a bash to the head, probably hadn't helped. We followed Shirley out into the hallway where they put on their heavy winter coats; Ernest pulled on his flat cap to hide the bump on his head before picking up his walking stick for the short walk to my car. I locked their house door and handed the keys to Shirley. Back at the car I opened the driver's door before reaching across and opening the passenger door for Ernest to climb in the back seat. That's when I found out that he wasn't used to travelling by car, and he certainly wasn't familiar with getting into the back seat of a two-door hatchback. I walked around the car and leaned into the passenger side and tilted the seat forward. 'Do you expect me to get in there?' he asked, pointing at the tiny gap that he would have to squeeze through.

'Yes, I'm afraid that's it, here let me help you.'

He handed Shirley his walking stick and I gripped his left arm to hold him steady. Then he tentatively stepped forward with his right foot. Within seconds he came to a stop, there was nowhere to put his left foot, he was stuck.

'Just hold on a minute Ernest,' I told him. 'I'll slide the seat forward to give you a bit more room.'

I moved the seat as far forward as it would go, allowing him more room for his other foot. He tried again, he leaned forward this time and managed to get both feet inside the car. Ernest was now almost bent over double but was unable to turn around and get his backside down on the seat. To make matters worse he couldn't bend any lower and his head was now wedged firmly against the roof of the car.

Shirley thought the whole thing was hilarious. 'Now who's a silly old cow?' she shouted. 'Look at the state of you, you've got yourself stuck haven't you, you daft old bugger.' Oh how she was enjoying the spectacle, leaning on the open door to watch her husband's struggle.

The old chap was never going to get in that back seat without some help, I'd have to do something to help him on his way. 'Here Ernest, let me give you a hand.' I leaned inside the car and squeezed my hand between the top of his flat cap and the roof of the car. Success, now with a bit of brute strength and ignorance from me and we would be on our way. I pushed firmly down on his head and at the same time pulled his shoulder backwards to force him into the rear seat.

He didn't appreciate my help and cried out in pain.

'Ahhh, your hurting me bleedin 'ed.'

'Oops sorry Ernest,' I replied. I had completely forgotten about his injured head. More amusement for Shirley who was now almost doubled over with laughter; well at least someone was finding it amusing.

At last Ernest was sat down. I tilted the passenger seat back to its normal position and Shirley plonked herself down. I slammed the passenger door shut before walking around the car and climbing into the driver's seat. At least there was some relief that the first obstacle was successfully overcome but at the same time I was dreading the prospect of getting Ernest out of the car at the Bridewell. With my seatbelt clipped in I turned on the ignition and moved off.

'Erm, what about our seatbelts?' asked Shirley.

I had forgotten all about that. 'Can't you fasten it yourself?' I asked.

'No, don't know how to, we usually go on t' bus.'

I pulled over at the side of the road, my patience rapidly running out. I leaned across Shirley to put on her seatbelt. It clicked into position easily enough but now for the difficult part. I turned round to check on Ernest who was still rubbing his sore head. 'Can you pass me your seatbelt Ernest?'

'What seatbelt?'

'That one behind your left shoulder.'

He managed to turn his head only a couple of inches; 'Can't see one lad, don't know where it is.' I could see it quite clearly but Ernest was unable to turn round properly. There was only one thing for it, I turned off the engine and climbed out of the car intending to fasten the seatbelt for him. A minute later I was squeezing into the back seat alongside him. I reached across him and pulled the seatbelt towards me, making sure that there was plenty of slack. Now to find the buckle, but there was no sign of it anywhere. I groped under his backside but it was no good. It must be underneath the seat somewhere, no doubt left there when the car was last valeted. This job was going from bad to worse. The thought of getting Ernest back out of the car and finding the seatbelt buckle was just too much for me.

'Do you really want a seatbelt on Ernest?' I asked. 'I promise that I'll drive really carefully and I won't crash so you don't really need it.'

'No you're all right lad, I wasn't really bothered anyway.'

'You're supposed to wear it,' chirped Shirley. 'I've seen it on telly, it was that Jimmy Saville, remember clunk-clip every trip, you can get fined if you don't wear it.'

Oh shut up you silly old bugger, well that's what I thought, but somehow I managed to bite my tongue. By now I was having a serious sense of humour failure.

After thirty minutes of very careful driving I pulled into the car park at the Bridewell, this was the part that I was really dreading. What a time for this to happen, just after midnight on a Saturday night. The place would be full of drunks, most of them under the age of twenty-five and here I was, turning up with a couple of pensioners. Given the choice I would park in the undercover garage, known as the 'van dock' and out of public view. Then we could sneak in unseen. But tonight there was already a van in there so I couldn't use it. I'd have to park in the outside car park and my 'prisoners' would be in full view of everyone. I cringed at the thought, this was going to be very embarrassing. I unclipped Shirley's seatbelt and we both climbed out of the car. She stood by the passenger door and watched intently as I reached inside and tugged at Ernest's arm to haul him out. It became a tug of war. The more I pulled, the more Shirley laughed and the more Ernest complained about his sore head. Five tortuous minutes of huffing and puffing and he was out. It was then a 20-yard walk towards the door to the Bridewell. I felt like I was taking my grandparents for a midnight walk.

I pressed the buzzer to gain entry. Damn. No response. We would be visible on a CCTV camera so when the custody staff heard the buzzer they would know I was waiting to come in. I pressed the buzzer again and waited for the door to be opened electronically. As soon as someone inside the building pressed the release button it should be a simple case of pushing the door open and walking through with my prisoners. But it wasn't happening this time, so I pressed the buzzer again. Then a voice came over the loud speaker: 'What do you want?'

Oh that's really funny. They knew exactly what I wanted. I had already told them all about it over the radio when I set off from Shipley. Someone in there was having a laugh, at my expense. 'Open this bloody door,' I demanded. 'I've got two prisoners from a domestic, stop messing about and let us in.'

Muffled laughter could be heard over the intercom. Shirley broke the silence: 'I thought they locked prisons to keep the people in,' she chuckled. 'But this lot 'ave locked us out.'

'It's not a prison, it's a police station and they'll let us in in a minute,' I replied through gritted teeth.

The laughter continued on the intercom. Inside, they could hear my conversation with Shirley and were having a jolly good laugh about it. Then, finally, I heard the lock disengage, one push and the door swung open. I ushered Shirley and Ernest inside and directed them to turn left into the waiting room, well that was a relief, it was completely empty. We walked into the long narrow room, furnished with just a polished wooden bench running along one wall. The normal procedure is that when entering this room the prisoners are told sit on the bench nearest to the door that they've just come through. The arresting officer stands alongside them. At the far end of the room another door leads through to a second, smaller room, containing the charge desk. Each time the custody staff receive a new prisoner those still waiting all shuffle a little further along the bench until it's their turn to be to be 'booked in' at the charge desk.

My elderly prisoners sat down on the wooden bench. Shirley was still quite giggly, treating her arrest as a good night out and determined to enjoy herself. Ernest was also happy now that he'd been released from the police car. Hard to believe that only two hours ago these two had been hitting each other. Their mood was contagious and I started to lose my earlier grumpiness.

They sat patiently, ten minutes passed and still we waited. I assumed that the custody staff were dealing with an awkward prisoner but the delay didn't matter anymore. These two were now chatting away quite happily and Shirley even asked if they could share the same cell. The atmosphere had definitely thawed between them, leaving me to wonder why they were here. Wasn't I was supposed to be one of the good guys? Surely my job is to lock up the bad guys. Well it wasn't working out that way tonight.

Eventually the booming shout of 'NEXT' indicated that it was our turn to go through to the charge desk. Ernest would go first. He struggled to his feet but on standing up he looked down at the bench behind him. Until then I hadn't notice anything untoward but Ernest now had a dark wet patch on the seat of his trousers. He wiped his hand on the wet patch before raising it to his nose to sniff his fingers. Screwing up his face in disgust he announced, 'It smells like piss, and I've been sat in it.'

I wasn't particularly surprised, it had happened many times before when a drunken prisoner decided to relieve himself on the bench. 'Yeah it might be piss,' I said, 'Probably another prisoner before we got here.'

Shirley hadn't yet moved, she leaned away from Ernest and for the first time I noticed that she was also sat in a large puddle. She looked across to Ernest, her hand held to her mouth to hold back her laughter. Then she confessed, 'You're right there, it is piss, it was me, I couldn't wait any longer so I've pissed myself, and you've been sat in it too.'

She laughed so much that I couldn't help joining in, even Ernest had a grin on his face. After fifty years of marriage this couple had probably had so many ups and downs that tonight's events were no more than a minor blip, by tomorrow it would all be forgotten. It was comforting to see that they were still able to share a joke, even in a place like this. A minute later the custody staff were equally amused when I told them about the domestic dispute and the damp patch on Ernest's trousers. The custody sergeant thought briefly about his responsibilities before telling me that he had little time for the new directives covering domestic disputes.

Nor did he want two drunken pensioners, one of whom suffered from incontinence, clogging up his cells. He shook his head in disbelief before telling me, 'Give them both an adult caution, and then get them out of here as quick as you can.'

Shirley was disappointed, she wasn't going to prison after all, wouldn't even spend a night in the police cells. She hadn't had so much excitement in years. By this time next week she'd be back to the same routine, sat watching the telly with only the dog and a bottle of brandy for company. Ernest would be back at the local pub getting drunk again, telling his mates about his arrest for belting his wife, but probably too embarrassed to say that she smashed his supper over his head.

Twenty minutes later a police van pulled into the car park. A lift back to Shipley was the least that I could do for them. But there was no way that I was letting them anywhere near my police car, one journey in a panda was more than enough.

CHAPTER 13

Bingo Caller

Being a copper is not all about arresting criminals, that would be far too simplistic and often doesn't tell the full story. Sometimes you deal with incidents that leave you with a heavy emotional burden to carry around. It's made worse when you know that a young man's life is falling apart, and it was probably your involvement that started his downfall.

In 1993 Paul Gardener was a bingo caller at Walker's bingo hall in Shipley. You would think that such a job was about the most innocent of all occupations, but sadly Paul had already fallen in with the wrong crowd, he was short of money and crime seemed an easy way out. My involvement began one evening after a report of theft at the bingo hall. I there met the owner of the business who told me the evening's takings had been stolen. It amounted to several hundred pounds, mostly in one pound coins. He started by showing me into the cash office. I examined the scene but there was no sign of a forced entry, suggesting that it was an inside job and a member of staff was involved. The only point of entry was through a locked fire door leading to the outside fire escape. The door was undamaged and had been opened by the key from the outside. There were only two sets of keys, I was told, the complainant had one set and the others were in the possession of his employee, Paul Gardener. It was no coincidence that Paul had been working in the cash office earlier in the evening. He had been alone at the time but had since finished work and had presumably gone home.

Paul didn't have a criminal record; he was eighteen years old and shared a council flat with his girlfriend, not far from the bingo hall. I obtained details for the crime report before making my way to Paul's flat. Outside I heard the sound of several voices coming from within. In those days we didn't worry too much about the legality of entering a property without a warrant so I tried the door handle, it was unlocked. I pushed the door open and walked straight in, stepping quickly through a small hallway and into the living room. Four startled faces turned to gawp at their unwelcome visitor. They sat in a circle on the floor, cross-legged, with a huge mound of one-pound coins at their feet, a look of disbelief and shock on each face. Not a word was spoken until I broke the silence.

'Hello lads, what are you lot up to then'?

Silence prevailed. I pointed down to the incriminating evidence. 'Been raiding someone's piggy bank then?' Still no reply, and crucially, no denial either. A couple of them turned away. Another looked down guiltily at the coins still in his hand. They must have known that when a uniformed copper walked into the room that their little game was up. I closed the door behind me, checked the kitchen and bedroom to confirm that there was no one else in the flat. These lads were too naive and too stunned to move, all just sat there hoping that the stolen money would disappear.

They were caught 'bang to rights'. It was a simple arrest and all the stolen money was recovered. Within minutes I was arranging for the van to transport the culprits back to the cells. Later that evening I interviewed Paul, he told me that his part in the crime had been to sneak outside with the spare keys and hand them to his friends. They waited until Paul finished his shift before entering with the keys and stealing the money. It was a very amateurish theft and one which was easily detected. The other three youths were all under the age of seventeen, none had any previous convictions, and during interview all admitted their guilt. Juvenile cautions followed and they were soon on their way home. Unfortunately for Paul he was slightly older than the others, and at eighteen was legally an adult. He was therefore charged with burglary before being released on bail.

The following night I spoke the owner of the bingo hall and told him what had happened at Paul's flat. As expected, Paul was sacked on the spot. In the weeks that followed Paul didn't know which way to turn. It would be months before his trial and during that time he struggled to obtain further employment, and soon became desperate for money.

Paul's life was now heading in a downward spiral. Within weeks I again had reason to arrest him. It was late at night, he and another youth were very drunk on cheap cider when they broke a window and entered a local school. It was a burglary which was destined to fail before it even began. Paul hoped to steal something which could be sold to pay his rent and buy food, but again it was a pathetic attempt. On climbing inside the building they inadvertently set off an audible burglar alarm. But they were too drunk to notice the ring of the alarm bell and rather than running away they remained on the premises, both wandering around aimlessly until I attended. I climbed in through the same window that they had used and found them hiding in one of the class-rooms, half-heartedly looking for an escape route. Another arrest followed but Paul was still on bail for the earlier incident, so this time he was refused bail and remanded into custody until his trial date. It turned out to be the last time that I ever spoke to this young man, someone whom I was starting to think of as a likable rogue.

Being remanded into custody must have been a real shock to Paul; his age dictated that he was no longer eligible to be detained at a Young Offenders' Institute, instead he went directly to an adult prison in Leeds. Armley is a prison which houses every category of inmates, from first timers like Paul through to long-term prisoners serving a life sentence for murder. Paul was straight in at the deep end, locked-up in a place where he would mix with hardened criminals after committing only two rather petty crimes.

By nature Paul was a reserved and quiet lad, at times he could be very shy and inoffensive, probably having more in common with the ladies at the bingo hall than with the

hardened inmates. He was small in height with a slim
build so he would soon be subject to bullying in the prison.
Following a period on remand he was returned to court
where he pleaded guilty and was sentenced to a short term in
prison. Armley would be his home for the remainder of that
sentence. He was there for three months but during that time
he got to know other criminals. I suspect he felt intimidated
and maybe sought protection in their company. Those
friendships may well have helped Paul survive in prison but
after his release there would be a heavy price to pay.

Back in Shipley the local council wasted little time in
repossessing his flat. Following his release Paul discovered
that he was now both homeless and pennyless. In the coming
weeks he took up residency in another rented flat, not in
the town of Shipley where he had the support of family
and friends, but on the top floor of a large terraced house in
Bradford. His circle of friends had changed dramatically
whilst he was in prison and it wasn't long before he was
associating with former cellmates. That was when his life
started to move in a new and sinister direction.

His new flat became known for drug dealing activities in
the district, and in particular heroin. There was no suggestion
that Paul was a user, or a dealer of heroin, but there was
suspicion that the drug was being sold from his flat. To make
things worse he wasn't the sort of lad who was capable either
physically or mentally of putting a stop to this lucrative trade.
His former cellmates were physically stronger and more
aggressive than him, and they were happy to use his place to
run their own lucrative business.

Always there in the background and watching what was
going on was Ian, Paul's younger brother. The brothers
were only two years apart, they had always been close when
growing up and there was still a strong bond between them.
Ian kept in regular contact with his older brother and became
a regular visitor to the flat. He saw his brother slide into the
murky world of drugs and criminality, wanted to help but
was powerless to rid Paul of the criminals who were likely to
get him sent back to prison. Ian could think of only one way
out of this crisis. Over the coming weeks he considered the

possibility of informing the police. He didn't want to be a
'grass' but he became convinced that there was no other way
to help his brother.

Ian was tormented by the problem. Paul was being dragged
into that seedy underworld of drugs and crime. Within days
Ian's mind was made up, he called in at the police station
and the information he provided was passed on to the drug
squad. A raid on the flat was planned.

On the day of the raid Paul was at home with Tommo,
one of his former cellmates. The drug squad officers quietly
gained entry to the outer door at street level. Once inside
they walked up the flights of stairs to the door of Paul's flat.
It was customary for them to force an entry quickly when
raiding premises so that the occupants would be taken by
surprise. This would stop them flushing the drugs, and therefore the evidence, straight down the toilet. The drug dealers
were aware of this procedure so they would usually reinforce
the door with extra locks and steel bars, hoping to delay any
forced entry by the police.

The officers gathered silently on the landing before
starting to smash down Paul's door, using door-rams and
sledge hammers. Inside, the frightened occupants heard
the commotion out on the landing and were thrown into a
state of instant panic, but this being a top floor flat their only
escape route was out on to the roof. In the kitchen was a
dormer-type window where extra rooms had been created
in the roof space. What had originally been a three-storied
house had been extended upwards to form a fourth floor in
the attic, maximizing the rental potential. By climbing out of
this dormer window they could step out onto the sloping
roof and hope to find an escape route. They were now some
40-feet above ground level, and far below, the yard had been
paved with flagstones. Every step was a dangerous move,
a steep slope with a covering of slippery moss growing on
the roofing slates. The roof extended in an unbroken line
from one end of the terrace to the other and there was no
easy way down.

Tommo led the way, directly followed by Paul himself.
They had made it out of the window and on to the sloping

roof with only seconds to spare before the police charged through the door. The two frightened young men ran across the slope, both desperately looking for a way down but there wasn't one. Tommo shouted that they would have to climb down one of the cast iron down pipes. But first they'd have the difficult task of reaching the pipe, which was hidden from view underneath the gutter. It would be a very frightening and dangerous manoeuvre to reach down and grab hold of the pipe below the eaves, not unlike climbing down an overhang on a cliff face whilst being unable to see where their feet were going; but they both knew that this pipe would be their only hope.

Paul crouched down on the roof and watched as Tommo went first. Somehow he carried out this tricky manoeuvre safely and within seconds he was shinning down the pipe to freedom. By now the drug squad officers had arrived at the dormer window and were looking out on to the roof. They saw Paul about 30 yards away. He was lying face down on the roof slates with his feet and legs dangling over the 40-foot drop. They watched helplessly as he desperately eased his body over the edge of the roof. Paul's hands were reaching under the gutter for the drain pipe. All he had to do was secure a good hand hold and he could then follow Tommo safely down to the ground.

But Paul's flailing hands missed the pipe by inches. He fell backwards, tumbling through the air. Tommo was halfway down by this time and watched his friend fall. Paul's body crashed into the top of a door canopy at basement level which spun him round before he landed on the ground with a dull thud. There was no movement, his body was contorted and broken; blood seeped from his nose and ears and formed dark red pools on the flagstones. Tommo continued his descent down the drain pipe before running straight past his friend, now only concerned about his own escape.

The officers witnessed this tragedy from the window. They ran back down the stairs to help Paul but sadly there was no sign of life. Tommo fled the scene, he showed no compassion for his injured and dying friend. Paul passed away in that backyard in Bradford. A search of the flat failed to find any illegal drugs, it appeared that there was no reason to run, they could have allowed the drug squad access to the flat without trying to escape.

Soon after this incident I was sent to Paul's flat to ensure that the premises remained undisturbed. It was now officially a crime scene and any evidence recovered would become part of the coroner's report. Paul's body had been removed before I arrived but I remember looking out of the dormer window into the backyard where he landed. A pool of blood was still visible on the ground. I tried to imagine the terrifying thoughts flashing through Paul's mind as he tumbled backwards through the air. I also tried to put myself in his brother's shoes and wondered how he must be feeling, and I felt true resentment towards Tommo. Unlike me, the officers from the Drug Squad didn't know Paul personally, they could probably remain more detached, and as the afternoon wore on I found that being there by myself, in that cold and soulless flat, was unbelievably depressing.

The cruel twist to this story was that Ian was trying to help his brother in the only way he could. He would feel responsible for his brother's death and will carry that burden with him. Paul's death touched me deeply. Within the space of only two years, I had seen a young man go from being an innocent bingo caller to paying the ultimate price in a Bradford backyard. The drug culture had claimed yet another victim.

CHAPTER 14

Crazy Pursuit

By 2001, after nearly two decades of driving a panda, I was looking for a change. It was a rather amusing little incident which finally convinced me that it was time to move on. Following a radio message I was on my way to a council house in Baildon, an address I knew all too well, and one which usually meant trouble.

Soon I was approaching the home of Julie and Steven King, a couple of drunkards who had often had violent domestic disputes. I'd been there many times before, and usually ended up arresting Steven for thumping his lovely wife. Not that she needed any protection from me. Julie was a formidable woman who was more than capable of looking after herself, a fact which I recently saw for myself when interviewing Steven at the police station. 'Look at this,' he demanded as he pulled down his shirt collar to reveal a hideous scar on his neck. He was showing me what was clearly a knife wound, which he claimed was caused by Julie when she stabbed him two months earlier. 'You don't do anything about that do you,' he complained.

I have to admit that I was shocked on seeing the state of his neck. 'Well, what do you expect us to do about it when you don't bother to report it at the time?' I replied.

But today was a Sunday morning, so hopefully they should both be sober. What intrigued me though was that Julie had specifically asked for me by name, that was most unusual. I parked up the car, knocked on their front door and waited, not knowing what sort of reception to expect.

'Ah, PC Watson, come in, would you like a cup of tea?' said Julie. I was taken aback, not at all what I expected. At this house I was usually greeted with drunken abuse rather than hospitality.

This was all very suspicious I thought. 'What exactly is it that you want from me?' I asked.

There was a cheeky grin on her face when she said, 'We want to ask a favour.'

Once I was sat down with a cup of tea she explained that she wanted my signature on their passport applications for their summer holiday to Benidorm.

'Well you have known us for over five years,' she stated. 'And it's not asking for a reference, just asks you to confirm that it's us on the photos. We thought about asking at the doctors' surgery but they charge a fiver each, and we can't ask a priest because we don't go to church, so Steve suggested asking you.'

Well she did have a point. I had known them for over five years, even if it was only to deal with their drunken fights, and like she said, I would not be giving a character reference. I shook my head in disbelief before taking out my pen and endorsing the forms and photographs. They would get their passports and maybe I would get a bit of peace when they were abroad. But when the criminal class are asking the copper who usually arrests them to sign their passport applications, then maybe it's time to move on. I needed a new challenge, but where to? Not as simple as it first sounds. I enjoyed working shifts and I also enjoyed being in uniform so my options were limited.

There had been possibilities of a move to other departments in the last few years. Some time ago I completed an attachment to the mounted section with the intention of working on horseback. It was a thoroughly enjoyable experience, but it was not to be. At the time that I was about to apply a cut in the police budget closed the stables at Bradford and the whole department was moved to Wakefield. Too far to travel for me, so sadly I gave up on the idea of a career on horseback.

The Dog Section seemed more promising. I started off with a couple of weeks working with a qualified dog handler. After a successful interview I went on a 'suitability course'. However, the trainer on that course turned out to be a bit of a plonker. 'Do as I say, rather than do what I do' was his motto. At the end of the course he deemed that all the candidates had failed to reach his very high, but unspecified standards. I was convinced that it was nothing more than the trainers protecting their own little empire but the result was the same, I was not going to be a dog handler.

My next favoured option was the Road Traffic Department, I enjoyed driving and thought that I could meet their high standards. It would mean working the same shifts, and I'd still be in uniform, two things which were important to me. Even more appealing was the fact that my own division had a vacancy, so if I passed all the courses and exams I would stay at Keighley, which suited me just fine.

Following a successful interview I started my attachment to the Road Traffic Department. For the next six months I was under the guidance of Phil who introduced me to the skills of advanced driving and the wider role of being a road traffic officer. There was a Road Traffic Law course and a written exam before I moved on to the Advanced Driving course. It was a four-week course where we often drove along twisting roads at ridiculously high speeds. There were other driving courses covering the skills and police tactics when taking part in 'pursuits' (which to me is just another name for a car chase).

It was a challenging period but by the end of the year the training was finished. There was no end to all the facts and figures crammed into my head, most of which were never likely to be used, but I did have the certificates confirming that I now had the required expertise. Eventually I was back in my own division and working as a traffic cop. Keighley is a huge geographical area extending from the inner cities of Bradford and Leeds through to Lancashire in one direction and North Yorkshire in the other. For a traffic cop there's no better place to work.

Despite my new job title I was still involved with the cut and thrust of instant response policing, but now I had specific responsibility for dealing with road traffic incidents.

It was an afternoon shift when I attended a briefing and heard the sergeant mention a stolen car in our area. My sort of job, so I listened with interest. A Toyota Corolla GT had been stolen overnight. I wrote down the details in my pocket book, definitely one to look for.

At about five that same afternoon I was driving along Hanover Street in the town centre. The street was busy with people making their way home from work or out doing last minute shopping. I was driving really slowly around town, nice and gently over the speed humps, having a good look round and mindful of pedestrians on both sides of the road. People walked with heads down and bags of shopping as they crossed from one side to the other, just like any other town centre anywhere in the country.

Then I saw it speeding towards me, must have been travelling at more than 50 miles an hour. The front wheels hit the speed bump so hard that they lifted completely off the road. As they crashed back down it was the turn of the rear wheels and they too became airborne. It was a small white hatchback, a Toyota Corolla GT. I didn't need to check the registration number, I knew instinctively that it had to be the stolen car mentioned on the briefing. It flashed past me but I had a good look at the occupants, four young Asian lads, none of them looking older than seventeen, the passengers laughing at the driver's recklessness, and thoroughly enjoying the ride.

I spun my car round in the width of the road, turned on the sirens and blue lights but the gap between us was increasing as I moved up through the gears. I accelerated hard, now gaining on them quickly, the noise from the sirens deafening as it bounced off the buildings. It's so loud that it's almost impossible to make yourself heard when calling Control. Pedestrians stop and stare, then step quickly away from the edge of the road, back onto the relative safety of the pavement.

I'm still gaining on them when they turn right into Cavendish Street, there's slow moving traffic in both directions but it's a wide road. Plenty of room for the Corolla to drive straight down the middle. The traffic lights at the bottom of Cavendish Street are showing a red light, it's a blind junction and now I'm starting to get worried. I can guess what this driver is going to do, and he doesn't plan to stop, not under any circumstances.

Throwing caution to the wind, he goes straight through the red light, deliberately indicates left but swings the car violently to the right. There's a car coming from his left, the driver jumps on his brakes, tyres screech and it skids to a stop. At the same time there's a huge foreign truck coming from his right. The truck driver looks over the top of the other cars and sounds his horn, it's even louder than my siren. Sounds like a klaxon on one of those big American trucks and probably illegal on British roads, but right now that's the least of my concerns. Luck is on the side of the thief and miraculously he gets through the congestion without crashing.

I slow down for the red lights, check both ways, it's clear, drivers have either heard my sirens or the klaxon on the truck and they've all stopped. The stolen car has opened up a gap again, now he's about a hundred yards ahead and turning left, away from town. At the junction he misjudges the bend and his nearside wheels slam into the kerb, the back end of the car bounces up in the air; he nearly lost it then, nearly crashed. I'm after him and back on his tail again, a moment to collect my thoughts and get onto the radio. I pass the details to Control and hope that there's other patrol cars in the area.

I can imagine how this will end. The Corolla is being driven with such recklessness that a crash is inevitable. And if these lads get half a chance they'll do a runner. No chance of arresting all four of them, they're likely to escape unless I can get some help quickly. The Corolla makes a left turn on to Parkwood Street, a long straight road with industrial units flanking both sides. But there are a couple of terraced streets and, worryingly, a junior school too. Alarm bells are ringing in my head, this is becoming far too dangerous and I really should slow down and abandon the pursuit. That's what I should do, but that would go against a copper's natural instincts, our job is to catch criminals, not allow them to escape. I decide to carry on for another minute and see what happens.

'Traffic calming' measures have recently been constructed along this road, sets of half barriers or 'chicanes' are built into the carriageway. The idea is that they allow traffic from alternating directions to have a right of way over the oncoming traffic. In theory all the traffic will be slowed down to make the road safer for pedestrians. But the driver of the Corolla had no such intention, he drives straight down the middle of the road, forcing oncoming cars to swerve out of his way. I follow at the same speed, 50, 60, 70 miles an hour, it was sheer madness. I should back off because I was now putting the public at risk but I keep going.

At the end of the road is a roundabout, the Corolla goes for the first exit and turns sharply to his left, too sharp, he loses control. The back end of his car slews round towards the middle of the road, both nearside wheels leave the road surface and spin wildly in mid air. He's up on two wheels and for a split second I thought that it would roll completely over. Instinctively the driver turns the steering wheel violently to the right and somehow the car lands back on all four wheels. A near-miss but it barely slows him down and he's soon accelerating away again.

We're now on another industrial road, Dalton Lane, heading back towards the town centre, if he makes it into town then I will definitely drop back. No choice really. I think the unthinkable, knowing that if he continues like this he'll end up killing someone, and it would be seen as my fault rather than his.

There's a sharp left-hand bend coming up and I'm right up his backside, hoping to force him into making a mistake before we get back into town. It's working, he's going into this bend far too quickly, he'll never get round at this speed. At the last possible second I hit the brakes, the gap between us instantly opens up and then, realising that he's going too fast he panics and jumps on the brakes. Too late. His wheels lock-up and he's skidding forward in a straight line, at the very point where the road bends sharply to the left. He crosses the centre white line and smashes into the back of a parked car on the other side of the road before coming to a grinding stop. All four doors on the Corolla are instantly thrown open; four youths emerge, one from each door, intending to run in four different directions. It's all happened in a split second and I'm still moving, braking heavily, my front wheels are on the verge of locking up, scrabbling for grip on the tarmac. I steer my car to the offside of the Corolla, hoping to block the escape route of the two lads exiting on that side of the car. I must try to arrest the driver, his arrest being far more important than that of his passengers. I skid to a stop alongside, trying to watch where they all run. I pass very close to two lads running from the offside doors, very close indeed, avoid hitting them by only a couple of inches.

Then I'm out and running, my car door left wide open, blue lights rotating and the siren still wailing. I have my sights on a target, 20 yards ahead but I'm sprinting for all I'm worth and gaining on him. He looks round and sees me and instantly stops, raising both hands above his head in a mock surrender. I grab hold of him by the scruff of the neck and tell him that he's under arrest. He doesn't wait for any questions, decides to get his excuse in first.

'It wasn't me, I was in the back, wasn't me driving.'

'Yeah course you were,' I replied. 'And I bet that you don't know the driver's name either, do you.'

'No, like I said I was in the back, the driver said it was his car, I didn't know it was nicked.'

He was lying, but what else should I expect? I hand-cuffed him and started walking him back towards my car, disappointed that the driver had escaped; and knowing that if this lad stuck to his story he would later be released without being charged. A minute later we were almost back at my car, but on looking ahead I saw that a surprise was waiting for me.

For some reason one of the other youths who ran off was stood by the front wing of my police car; surely he wouldn't just stand there and wait for my return? He looked anxious, maybe even in pain, shuffling his feet about; well at least he was shuffling his left foot, his right foot wasn't moving. He was leaning forward with both hands resting on the bonnet of my car. The cheeky bugger, what's he up to I wondered. He had his back to me and hadn't seen me yet. I looked a bit closer, his hands were clenched into fists and he started banging them aggressively down on the car bonnet. I recognised him, tall and slim, with the usual clothing, blue hoody, dark blue jogger bottoms and white trainers.

No wonder I recognised him, he was the driver! But why hadn't he run away like the others? He'd had a chance to get clean away, I was baffled. I looked again at his white trainers, there was his left foot, stamping down onto the road. His right foot was … well fancy that … his right foot was nowhere to be seen. It was squashed under the wheel of my car, he was trapped, the poor lad's foot was now as flat as a pancake!

I was only a few yards away when he looked round and saw me for the first time, now he started thumping his fists down onto the car bonnet with more force.

'Move this fucking car you bastard,' he screamed, 'its bleeding killing me, get it off my fucking foot.'

I ambled slowly towards him, casually holding the hand-cuffs securing prisoner number one. Yes, this was certainly a surprise, and a very pleasant one at that. I tried not to laugh too much at his misfortune, no, really I didn't even try to hide my amusement, instead I was determined to enjoy it.

'Ello, ello, ello, and what have we got 'ere?' I asked in my best pantomime voice.

'Move this car NOW,' he shouted.

I ignored his abusive demands and continued to mock him. 'And wot 'ave you been up to young man, I'll bet that you've been trying to kick my car, and now you've got your foot stuck under my wheel haven't you. You're a very naughty little boy.'

'Ahh get it off … Now … It's fucking killing me.'

'Now, now, now, swearing won't help will it now.'

Oh how I was enjoying this moment, and even if no-one else found my pantomime character quite so amusing I just couldn't help myself. I continued to mock his bad luck. 'Don't you know that it's a crime to kick a police car? You could get yourself arrested for that, young man.'

By now prisoner number one was struggling to hide the smirk on his face, although he did at least try to conceal it from his unfortunate friend. I could well imagine that this young thief would be in some discomfort, I was driving the big Volvo T5 estate car, about two tons of metal with a massive engine under the bonnet. At this very moment he must have at least a quarter of that weight bearing down on his right foot. He continued to bang his fists down on the car bonnet, then he introduced a bit of variety by head-butting the car between the banging of his fists. His screaming and abusive language continued unabated.

'Get it off you bastard, you've done this on purpose.'

I hadn't done it on purpose, but I certainly wish that I had. I really was rather proud that I had somehow managed to bring my car to a stop in such a fortuitous position. Despite his protests I was in no hurry to move the police car. The pantomime continued for another minute or so until I realised that I was pushing my luck just a bit too far. Still no sign of any colleagues to back me up. I was rather vulnerable with a small but hostile crowd starting to gather round. The local residents heard the crash and my sirens and came out of their houses to see the spectacle. In that area I was definitely the outsider so it was time for me to be serious for once.

I'd need to reverse my car off this lad's foot without giving him the chance to run away. Not as straightforward as it sounds because right now I didn't know if he was still capable of running away. I thought about taking my handcuffs off the other lad so I could cuff the lad I named 'flatfoot' instead, but that wasn't without some risk.

I could do with some help but there was still no sign of any back-up. The crowd were getting agitated, couldn't stall for time any longer so I'd have to deal with this on my own. I sat the handcuffed prisoner number one in the back seat of my car intending to reverse off the other lad's foot. But as my backside landed on the driver's seat the screaming outside suddenly intensified in volume.

'Ahh, you bastard you're doing that on purpose.'

'Oops sorry,' I shouted back, suddenly aware that the weight on his foot had just increased by a further thirteen stones when I flopped down into the drivers seat. 'Sorry lad but I have to sit in the car to reverse it off your foot.'

I decided to remove the cuffs from prisoner number one, hoping that he wouldn't try to do a runner, and anyway I had little choice. I got out of the car and approached flatfoot. He was now laid with his upper body draped right across the bonnet of my police car. He'd given up with his act of bravado and was now openly crying and blubbering. I handcuffed his wrists behind his back and then climbed back into the driver's seat. More abuse and screaming when my backside landed on the seat for a second time. Ignoring his screams I started the engine and slowly, gently even, reversed the car off his foot. Would he try to run away even though he was handcuffed? No chance. He simply collapsed into the road, curled up in the fetal position and laid there crying like a baby.

Half a minute later I was picking him up from the ground when I heard the sound of police sirens. My back-up was here at last. They could have the dubious task of dealing with the angry mob, several of whom now demanding my collar number and screaming about police brutality. My colleagues would complete the paperwork for the collision and make a search of the area for the two lads who had escaped.

I set off back towards the police station, my two prisoners sat alongside each other on the back seat. Two prisoners and a stolen car recovered, not a bad result. I was rather pleased and couldn't resist winding up flatfoot.

'Well, it's not every day that I have a volunteer wanting to be arrested, someone who is just waiting at my police car for me to come along and lock him up.'

'Get fucked,' was his delicate reply.

But his mate saw the funny side; after all he was unlikely to be charged with any offence and he'd be out of the cells and back on the streets within hours.

'You've got to admit it Jaz,' said prisoner number one, 'It was funny when that cop car squashed your foot.'

'You can get fucked too,' replied flatfoot.

I chuckled at this exchange, as did prisoner number one, only flatfoot failed to find it quite so funny.

I would be busy for the rest of the day, two prisoners to take to the cells, get them booked into custody and complete all the paperwork. Interviews would take place sometime later in the day. But first I would be accompanying flatfoot to the local hospital.

CHAPTER 15

Leading by Example

Billy Blunder was not his real name, but the reason for the change will soon become clear. Billy first came into the police as a special constable (which means that he was a volunteer for a few hours each week and didn't get paid). And despite his obvious enthusiasm he was quickly marked down as a strange character. He was small in height, rather rotund and the owner of a round face with a spotty complexion; and he walked on the balls of his feet so he appeared to bounce along rather than walk.

Billy eventually achieved his lifelong ambition when he was appointed to the regular police, and then he was posted onto my shift at Bradford. He had a gritty determination to succeed in the job and soon passed the promotion exams. Then horror of horrors, he became a sergeant on my shift. By this time I was in the Road Traffic Department so although I worked closely with him I was spared the ordeal of having him as my supervisor.

Billy was soon in charge of a team of very young and inexperienced officers, ideal for a bloke who liked to create the right sort of impression. It was also important for Billy to be liked and thought of as 'one of the lads' on the team, probably the sort of bloke who was bullied as a child. Such character traits got him into trouble, as the next two stories demonstrate.

It was a night shift and I was out and about on patrol in the Area Road Traffic car. Sometime after midnight I saw a black Ford Fiesta speeding through a residential area of Shipley. I stopped at a junction and it sped past, giving me the chance to have a good look at the occupants. They were two young lads who both deliberately looked the other way, usually an indication that they had something to hide and a sure sign that they were up to no good. I pulled out behind them and turned on the siren and blue lights. Better check them out and see what they were up to. But they had no intention of slowing down or stopping. The driver hit the gas pedal and accelerated away. A quick radio call to Control revealed that it was a stolen car and the chase was on. I followed closely behind, expecting them to abandon the car at any minute and do a runner, that would be their best chance of getting away. The driving was now very erratic, too many risks being taken for this chase to last much longer.

The pursuit turned out to be even shorter than I expected, within a minute the joyrider went straight across the carriage-way and crashed head on into a drystone wall. The wrecked car was abandoned but the occupants were out in an instant and running like hell. They turned off the main road and sprinted into the darkness along a narrow farm track. Unbeknown to these lads, both sides of the track was lined with barbed wire and a thick hedgerow, there would be no escape. Still in my car I sped along the track after them, my wing mirrors scraping the hedgerow on either side, gaining on them with every second, only a few yards behind now. They looked back, terrified that I was going to run them down.

There's no escape lads, I said aloud, time to stop running and give yourselves up. But at the last possible second they hurled themselves off the track and dived head first through the barbed wire, and into the hedgerow. I jumped on the brakes, skidded to a stop and was out of my car and after them. They very nearly made it, almost escaped, but I reached through the fence and managed to grab the clothing of one lad who was tangled up in the barbed wire. I dragged him back on to the track, arrested him and pushed him into the back seat of my car. The other lad had been too quick for me. He'd made it through the hedgerow and disappeared into the night. Not much hope of finding him, but at least I had one prisoner.

With the lad safely locked in the police car I carefully leaned over the fence to look beyond the hedgerow. Difficult to see much in the dark, but my torch beam picked out a steep drop. I was surprised to see that the ground fell away almost vertically, as though the land had been excavated by a JCB digger or a bulldozer. I'd never noticed this drop before so I figured that it must have been done very recently. The land at the bottom of the slope was now used as a storage compound for dozens of trucks and trailers. The other lad could be anywhere by now, maybe hiding under a wagon or possibly running straight through and out of the other side. Still, there was little that I could do about it, not yet anyway. I'd have to wait until some back-up arrived, then I'd climb down and check it out for myself.

Within minutes another police car turned off the road and into the farm track, the driver had heard my radio commentary and had come to help. It was Louise, a young female officer who was out on patrol by herself, and just the sort of officer that Billy would want to impress.

'Hi Lou,' I greeted her as she hurried out of her car, 'Will you do me a favour and watch that prisoner in the back of my car? Another lad has climbed through this hedgerow and run off. I want to have a look for him.'

'Yeah, no problem Dave, I'll keep my eye on this lad.'

There was still a slim chance of finding the other lad, especially if he had decided to hide rather than keep running. I climbed through the hedgerow and over the barbed wire. Now I stood precariously on the edge of a very steep drop, about 20-feet deep and nearly vertical. Rather worryingly, the slope was loose and with little to hold it in place. It would be a difficult descent but the car thief had made it down so I had to give it a go. I started down, carefully picked my steps, trying to stand on the odd boulder sticking out or grabbing hold of the occasional tree root. A minute later I was nearly halfway down when my feet suddenly slipped from under me. I careered down the slope but somehow remained upright, almost in a skiing position. Landing heavily at the bottom, somehow I stayed on my feet, though my shoes and socks were now full of soil. Moments later I had emptied out the soil and was starting to search the compound.

It was hopeless, there was no sign of the other lad and within ten minutes I was ready to give up the search. I'd have to find a better way out of there, no chance of climbing out the way I came in, that would be damned near impossible. Then, much to my surprise I heard the sound of Billy's voice on the radio. I hadn't seen anything of him yet but it sounded like he was just entering the compound to search another section. His radio message continued by saying that his entrance was apparently not quite as elegant as mine had been but he had come to help me. A strange remark to make but he didn't give any further details and I thought no more about it.

But Billy had taken the trouble to come and help so the least I could do was wait for him to join me. A couple of minutes later we were both checking the whole compound again but the suspect still wasn't found. We finally gave up and decided that our suspect must have escaped. Billy and I parted company, deciding that we would both find our own ways back to our respective cars. I walked around the perimeter wall until I found an easier place to climb out. It was then a short walk to the farm track where I left my car with Louise guarding my prisoner.

On the unlit farm track I turned on my torch. The beam picked out Louise. She was stood, or should I say, crouched, at the side of the car; at first I thought she was crying as she was almost doubled over. I rushed towards her, suddenly concerned as horrible thoughts flashed through my head. Maybe the prisoner had attacked Louise and run away. Then on reaching her, I realised that she was unable to speak, and it wasn't because she was crying. It was because she was in fits of hysterical and uncontrollable laughter, and she had been like this for several minutes, ever since Billy first climbed down the slope into the compound.

Slowly she regained a little composure and explained what happened. Shortly after I went through the hedgerow Billy came bounding along the track. Without pausing for breath, he scrambled over the barbed wire fence and through the hedge where, for the first time, he looked down at the steep drop into the compound. This was going to be much more difficult than he first thought, but Billy was not one to shirk such a challenge. But it was pitch black and he would need a torch to see where he was going. And if Billy was going to the assistance of one of his officers then he wanted an audience, so he told Louise to lean over the fence and shine her torch for him as he climbed down. After a quick assessment of the slope he decided that the best way down was to cling on to a thin tree root exposed by the recent excavation. He would use the tree root as a climbing rope. That would allow him to lean out backwards in the classical abseil position and he could descend the slope and come to my assistance. He had done this sort of abseil many times before as a boy scout, he informed Louise. What better way for Billy to impress his junior officers than to abseil down into the blackness whilst in the spotlight of a powerful hand torch.

It seemed that his plan was going to work, well at least it did for about the first three feet. Billy confidently leaned back and let the tree root take the strain. Slowly he edged over the drop whilst clinging on to the tree root. Gradually he applied more weight onto his makeshift climbing rope, he took one step backwards, then another, only 15 feet to go. Then disaster struck, without warning the root suddenly snapped! Billy tumbled over backwards and plummeted down the slope, almost in free-fall until his leg snagged on another tree root and spun him round in a perfect somersault. He landed at the bottom with a thud, flat on his back in the dusty compound. Now he was severely winded and covered from head to foot in soil and green stains from the vegetation. Louise of course had witnessed all this and although she was dying to laugh she simply dare not do so, after all Billy was her sergeant. Struggling to hold back the laughter, she somehow managed to shout down, 'Are you alright Sergeant?'

'Yes, yes I'm fine,' he replied. Now feeling flustered and embarrassed he rose slowly to his feet and brushed himself down. Louise suppressed her laughter until he had moved away but then could contain herself no longer. But Billy wasn't the sort of man to let such a triviality deter him from doing his job, so after getting his breath back he was once again ready for action, and started looking around to find me. That was when he passed the radio message about his entrance into the compound lacking elegance. This incident would not have been nearly so amusing had it been anyone other than Billy, but his personality almost demands that colleagues find the story so entertaining.

The second incident took place in the car park of Bingley police station. On that particular night Billy was out on patrol driving the public order van. Once again his crew were young and inexperienced officers, and as usual, he tried to impress them with his vast knowledge and experience. Nick sat in the back of the van, bored by Billy's tales of daring-do. He asked if they could go back to the police station as he needed to use the toilet. For Billy this was another opportunity to demonstrate his own importance. Rather than drive back to Bradford, he decided they would use the facilities at Bingley police station instead. Bingley is only manned during the day and the building was closed and locked up at that time of night. But Billy would demonstrate the importance of his rank because he alone had the privilege of knowing the alarm code.

Bingley police station is a Victorian, stone-built traditional station. A set of wooden stocks still exist within the grounds, although, sadly no longer in use. It has a high stone boundary wall with ornate stone pillars on either side of the car park entrance. Until a few years ago a stone sphere sat on top of each one of these pillars but vandals had pushed them off and they were now abandoned under the fire escape.

Soon the van pulled into the spacious car park and Billy proudly accessed the building using the security code known only to him. Then he and Nick went inside to make use of the facilities. The remaining officers, who had been cramped up in the back of the van for hours, decided to get out and stretch their legs by strolling around the car park. The long abandoned stone spheres were spotted lying under the fire escape, and conveniently they just happened to be a very similar size to a football, a chance to play a practical joke on their mate they thought. One of the stone spheres was rolled out towards the van, and there it waited for Nick.

Within minutes Nick left the police station and was on his way back to the van. He walked towards Alan who was now stood with his foot resting on the stone sphere. Alan rolled the 'ball' towards him, hoping that Nick would think it was a genuine football and give it a good hearty kick. It would probably bruise Nick's toes but that would be a small price to pay for everyone having a good laugh at his misfortune.

But Nick wasn't that stupid, this ball was clearly very heavy, didn't roll like a real football and he guessed that his colleagues were trying to set him up. With a smile on his face he walked straight past it and climbed back into the van. Billy was last to leave the building, busy setting the security alarm, then as he walked across the car park the 'football' was rolled towards him. Billy is noted for having very poor eyesight, something which on this occasion was going to cost him dearly. He obviously thought that the stone sphere looked like a real football. So picking up his pace he sprinted the last few steps and brought his right leg back in preparation for his penalty kick. He swung his leg forward with real force, expecting to give the stone sphere an almighty boot. Everyone watched with bated breath and just before Billy's toes connected with the 'ball' he is reputed to have shouted 'HAVE IT!' at the top of his voice.

The stone sphere probably weighed a couple of hundred pounds, Yorkshire's finest millstone grit. He made a beautiful, full-blooded connection and had it been a real football it would have flown for miles. However, the stone merely rolled forward a few inches. Billy however screamed out in pain, hopping up and down and clutching his bruised toes. Everyone else fell about laughing, hardly able to believe what they had just seen. Billy hobbled back to the van and demanded to know who was responsible but, predictably, he was met by a wall of silence.

Billy Blunder has a heart of gold, the sort of bloke who would always try to help his officers, although as these tales demonstrate, his methods could be rather unconventional. I have little doubt that he was soon regarded as one of the real characters in the job, the sort of bloke whose reputation preceded him wherever he went.

CHAPTER 16

Wheel Clampers

'Oh no, not again,' I replied into the radio. 'Those people are really starting to get on my nerves, they're nothing but a bloody nuisance.'

I was responding to a radio message from Control. The notorious wheel clampers at the privately-owned 'pay and display' car park in Haworth were back to their usual tricks. The car park would be packed. It was a fine August day and hundreds of tourists would be visiting the Worth Valley Steam Railway where *The Railway Children* was filmed years ago. There would also be the usual hordes of people following the history of the Brontë sisters at the museum. I made my way to the police contact point, currently housed in a discrete and rather homely little cottage in the centre of the village. Waiting there to meet me was Mrs Crawford who had called at the contact point after her car had been clamped.

I parked outside, locked up my car and walked in. The village was too quiet to have regular police officers working there, instead a couple of elderly volunteers did their best to help, a kindly couple who provided tea and sympathy, but quite unable to resolve this problem themselves. The first volunteer informed me that such incidents were now becoming a daily problem and something should be done about it. It obviously wasn't only me who was getting fed up with the dubious practices of the wheel clampers. I went through to another small office, probably a sitting room before this cottage became the police contact point.

Mrs Crawford was sat with a cup of tea in her hand. An elderly lady, perhaps in her seventies and visibly upset.

I introduced myself and sat alongside her, couldn't help but notice that her hands were still shaking. On a small settee sat another elderly couple, surprisingly both looked somewhat older than Mrs Crawford. She introduced them as her relatives and they had been passengers in her car. I listened patiently as Mrs Crawford explained what had happened. Earlier today she drove to Haworth from her home at York intending to take her aunt and uncle for a day out. After a journey of over an hour they arrived in the village and she parked in the pay and display car park. After paying the parking fee the three of them made for the centre of the village to visit the Brontë museum. That was followed by a short walk around the numerous gift shops and the day would finish with afternoon tea in one of the cafes.

It was a pleasant afternoon out, well it was until they returned to her car, to find that it was now clamped. Mrs Crawford was at first rather puzzled by this, she had paid the parking fee for two hours and they still had twenty minutes remaining on the ticket. She went across to the wooden hut used as an office by the wheel clamper and tried to explain. But he wasn't interested in her explanation and insisted that she'd have to pay a fine of £60 for the clamp to be removed. This was because her ticket had been left face down on the dashboard and that, he claimed, was against the rules.

It was a familiar story. The businessman who happens to own the land used as a car park treads a very fine line between what is, and what is not lawful. I knew from past experience that he wouldn't be there himself. No, he's far too grand for such menial work. Instead he employs a number of men who bear a close resemblance to a bunch of thugs. They do the owner's dirty work and are paid on a 'commission only' basis so it's their own interest to clamp as many cars as possible. The slightest breach, or infringement of 'The Rules' will result in a wheel clamp being slapped on within seconds.

I already anticipated problems with this job and suggested to Mrs Crawford that her relatives should remain at the police contact point. She could accompany me to the car park where we would try to resolve the problem. She explained that she didn't have £60 in cash and had tried to pay the fine with a cheque. Her intention had been to simply pay up and leave for home without contacting the police but the wheel clamper had refused to accept her cheque.

My heart went out for this sweet old lady, she was the victim and yet she was still prepared to pay a fine to a person who, in my opinion was little more than a crook. The clamper was sat in his battered old van. It was parked alongside a timber shed which had its door wide open. Inside was a pile of unused wheel clamps littering the floor. No doubt he was just itching to get those clamps slapped on other cars.

Mrs Crawford's car was exactly as she had described, a bright yellow wheel clamp now firmly locked onto the front off-side wheel. She opened the car door and handed me the parking ticket from the dashboard, it confirmed everything she'd told me. Hopefully the clamper would listen to reason and remove the clamp so that this lady could take her relatives home. After all, it wasn't as though she hadn't paid to park there. Nor had she overstayed her allotted time, in fact she had returned to the car park before the due time.

The clamper was now strutting towards us. A rough, scruffy-looking individual with long greasy hair, tall and lean with a few days growth of stubble on his scrawny face and neck, self-inflicted tattoos on his hands, wrists and neck; and in need of a good wash. Little wonder that Mrs Crawford had been frightened by him, he was a fearful sight. Maybe I should appeal to his better nature.

'This lady has a valid parking ticket,' I told him. 'Can't you just remove the clamp and let her go home?' I showed him her ticket. 'Look, she's paid to park here.'

'No, sorry boss. Can't do that,' he replied, 'Her ticket was face down, that's not allowed, and I can prove it, I've photographed it on my mobile if you want to see.'

The word 'boss' he used when addressing me suggested that he'd spent time in prison. It's a term that inmates use when addressing anyone in authority, and it seems that the habit stays with them long after their release. Maybe he wasn't as stupid as he looked either, he'd had the foresight to photograph the ticket in situ so that it couldn't be disputed later. This might prove more difficult to resolve than I first thought.

I tried again. 'Yes, okay. I don't need to see the photograph, I believe you about the ticket being face down, but she has still paid for the ticket hasn't she?'

'Yes boss but she broke the rules, and I'm not allowed to take the clamp off until I've been paid.'

Not allowed by whom, I wondered, no one else would ever know, this man was determined to get his money.

'How is she supposed to know all the rules?' I asked, seemed like a reasonable question to me. Then I continued, 'This is nothing but a genuine mistake, and you know it is.'

He pointed across the car park towards the ticket machine, it was fixed to a large notice board. 'All the rules are printed on that board so she can't say that she didn't see 'em, she must 'ave been stood looking at 'em when she bought her ticket.'

Reluctantly I had to accept that he was right. All the rules were there to be seen but who would spend several minutes reading through all the rules and regulation when buying a parking ticket? It was totally unreasonable but this bloke had all the answers and unfortunately he had the law on his side too, sadly it didn't matter how unfair that law may be. Worst of all he had this lady over a barrel, and there wasn't a thing that I could do about it. I tried again.

'Right, how are we going to sort this out?'

'I've told you boss, that clamp stays on till she pays up.'

'But she hasn't got £60 in cash and I understand that you won't accept a cheque.'

'Can't accept cheques boss, or people would just put a stop on them at the bank when their car was released.'

Yes, this bloke definitely had all the answers.

'I'll take a credit card,' he then told me. 'I've got a swipe machine in my van but she says that she doesn't 'ave one.' His tone suggested that he didn't believe Mrs Crawford, even though many people of her generation don't possess credit cards.

'Well how do we resolve this then?' I asked, exasperated with the idiot stood before me.

'She'll 'ave to go home on the bus and get the money won't she?' he suggested.

'But I live nearly 50 miles away in York and I've got two elderly relatives with me,' explained Mrs Crawford.

He just shrugged his shoulders. 'Not my problem love.'

What an absolute bastard this bloke was turning out to be. Then he hit her with the final blow.

'And if you can't get back here before we close today we'll take the car to a compound. Then it costs £120 to be released.'

'Why's that?' I asked.

'Cause if we leave the car here then some people would come back during the night and cut the clamp off to drive away wouldn't they?'

I was sure that I'd exhausted every avenue I could think of. It was like banging my head against a brick wall, and as difficult as it was to accept, I was beaten. Beaten by an uncouth thug who knew exactly how to work the system to his advantage. I took Mrs Crawford to one side and explained the hopelessness of the situation. She had a tear in her eye, but her pride and dignity prevailed, she wasn't going to cry in front of the wheel clamper.

'Is there anyone at home who could bring you the money?' I asked.

'There's only my husband but he's got MS and he's in a wheelchair. My sister's looking after him today to give me a break, that's why we came here, we were hoping to have a nice day out.' Her 'nice day out' was turning into a nightmare.

'You wait here love, I'll just go have another word with the clamper,' I told her. Have a word with him, I'd rather go over there and punch his lights out, but I suppose that that would be against the rules too.

He was back in his battered van, I pulled open the door and leaned inside. I was angry now and didn't care if it showed. 'Where's that credit card swipe machine of yours?'

'Right boss, getting somewhere now are we?' he chuckled to himself. 'Suddenly found her card then?' he suggested. 'You can tell when people are trying it on when you've done

this job as long as me.' His supercilious smile revealed a row
of rotten brown teeth.

'No, she hasn't got a credit card,' I told him. 'I'm going
to give you mine. I'll pay the fine so that you'll release her
car. And if there are ever any unauthorized payments on my
card I'll be back here to lock you up, and don't you ever
forget that.'

His earlier confident and arrogant manner was now somewhat subdued but he still couldn't resist having a final dig
at me.

'Well I never thought I'd see a copper paying someone
else's parking ticket out of his own pocket, I reckon you must
be a bit soft in the head.'

I handed him my credit card which he expertly swiped
before handing me the machine and asking for my signature.
I was not happy about giving details of my card but under the
circumstances there was no alternative. He handed me back
my card and I slammed the van door shut before walking
across to Mrs Crawford to tell her how the problem had
been resolved. A minute later there was a tear in her eye, she
turned away so it wouldn't be seen by the clamper. He didn't
care, now busy removing the clamp, happy that he'd made
his day's wage.

Mrs Crawford assured me that she would write to me
and send the money, I didn't have the slightest doubt that
she would. I gave her my details and she was finally able
to retrieve her car. I watched her drive from the car park to
collect her relatives from the police contact point for what
would be a miserable drive back to York.

As I drove away I pondered over what I should tell
Control. They have to record every result on the computer
log which all police staff have access to. I decided to leave the
result as being rather vague: 'The parking fee has been paid,'
I reported. 'And Mrs Crawford has now got her car back.'
That would have to do. I could well imagine that if some of
my colleagues knew the truth that they would agree with the
wheel clamper; I was becoming 'soft in the head' and I'd be
ridiculed back at the station.

If nothing else I'd done my good deed for the day, but inside I was still angry and frustrated about the antics of the wheel clamper. It just wasn't right, I mused, when people like him can bully such kind and gentle people like Mrs Crawford. I was still mulling over these thoughts some 20 minutes later when I again heard my call sign on the radio.

'Whisky Hotel Three Six, I'm sorry about this but can you go straight back to that car park again, we've had another call, this time from a man called Mr Slade, he say's that he's the wheel clamper and now he's having trouble with a female. He's say's that she's damaged his van.'

I really didn't want to go back there again but I had little choice, although I did find it rather intriguing to hear that Slade was now the complainant!

Within five minutes I was back there. The wheel clamper's van was now blocking the entrance to the car park. Already three cars waited on the roadway to enter and another two waited to leave. But it seemed that the belligerent wheel clamper was refusing to move his van out of the way. I parked up and walked towards Slade's van. He saw me coming and climbed out to join me. His whole demeanour was very different now, he appeared tense and agitated. His earlier arrogance and confidence had deserted him. In fact he was pacing about like a cat on a hot-tin roof and before I said a word he just blurted out, 'It's them two.'

He pointed towards an old Ford Mondeo. Two women were sat in the car and as he spoke they stepped out and walked towards us. The woman from the driver's seat was tall and heavily-built. She marched purposely towards us, an angry look on her face and she aggressively pointed at Slade.

'That miserable little shit tried to clamp my car,' she said. 'And I've got a ticket here to show that I've paid, look it's here, if you want to see it.'

She was as tall as me and must have weighed in at nearly twenty stones, quite a sight in her industrial overalls and heavy black boots. The second woman was of a similar size and appearance, which made me think that they could be sisters. I could almost see these two in a wrestling ring as a formidable heavyweight tag-team. Certainly not the sort of women to be trifled with.

The first woman thrust the ticket in my direction then stood and faced me with arms folded across her ample bosom. She looked over my shoulder at Slade and glared at him. I took the ticket from her and checked the details, noticed her big meaty fists that were used to manual work. She was certainly no delicate little lady like Mrs Crawford. It amused me to think that Slade had met his match, he wouldn't intimidate this woman like he did Mrs Crawford. If anything it was the other way round with Slade being the frightened victim, I almost felt a tinge of sympathy for him.

'What's your name love?' I asked.

'Roof,' she snarled. 'But I don't want 'im knowing my name.' She nodded towards Slade. 'Roof?' I enquired, 'Is that what you said?' 'Yes it's Roof, is there summat wrong with your 'earing?' Maybe there was something wrong with my hearing, who would ever name their daughter Roof, what a ridiculous name. Then the penny suddenly dropped, her name couldn't possibly be Roof, it must be Ruth but she definitely pronounced it as Roof. Best to stay on the right side of this woman or she might thump me!

'Yes, I'm sorry Ruth, but you're right, my hearing isn't too good.' I glanced across at Slade and saw that he was busy looking down at the ground, not daring to return her stare.

'He won't find out who you are Ruth, but will you and your friend please return to your car until I find out what's happened?'

She gave me a nod. 'That's alright then int it,' she stated. I was curious about this woman so before she walked away I spoke to her again. 'I don't think you're local are you, where are you from?'

'We're from 'Alifax, just come 'ere to see a mate, and that little git tried to rip me off din't he.'

I was beginning to understand the dialect now. Ruth was from the nearby town of Halifax, the dialect became easier to understand after the first couple of minutes. Both women stomped off and as Ruth was about to get in the driver's seat of her car she turned again and looked at Slade with staring eyes and her jaw set aggressively. She was definitely trying to frighten him, oh how his fortunes had changed.

Now that Ruth was safely out of Slade's way he had the confidence to speak more freely. He said that she paid for only one hour but left her car parked for 65 minutes. By overstaying her allocated time she was in breach of 'the rules' and would have to pay the fine. Apparently he had been about to clamp her car when she returned. But being such a reasonable sort of chap he gave her the opportunity of paying the £60 fine. She refused and that's when he then tried to fit the wheel clamp. He bent down at her front wheel to fit the clamp but she climbed into the driver's seat and reversed her car away, nearly squashing his fingers in the process. Slade was determined to have his money. He ran to his van and parked it across the entrance of the car park to stop her leaving.

That made Ruth even more angry, as far as she was concerned she had paid the parking fee and this little creep was trying to get more money out of her. Apparently both women got out of their car intending to give Slade a good hiding. They charged towards his van and tried to drag the doors open. Slade was forced to admit to me, rather embarrassingly, that fearing for his safety he locked himself inside. The mad woman was going berserk, he told me, all her self-control was now gone and she blew her top. Within seconds she was laying into his van with her steel toe-cap boots. The now petrified clamper called 999 from the safety of his van and reported that two women were attacking him!

Poor Mr Slade was obviously deeply uncomfortable when telling this story. It probably didn't help when he saw the grin on my face. It was the best thing I'd heard all day and left me feeling much happier.

'So are you telling me that there is a parking fine of £60 still outstanding?' I finally asked.

'Yes, that's right, there's still sixty quid to pay,' he replied.

He probably saw a glimmer of hope. Maybe I would do his dirty work and get the money from Ruth. Or perhaps I would take the easy option and hand over my own credit card and pay him another sixty quid. After all he already knew that I was soft in the head! Today could still turn out to be a good day for him, especially if someone else paid the fine, namely yours truly.

'Have you taken a photograph to record the time when she came back to the car?' I asked.

'No, I never got the bleedin' chance, I told you, the mad cow nearly run me over.'

'So I take it that there's no evidence to confirm that she overstayed her permitted time then?'

He was slowly getting the idea that he was flogging a dead horse this time. He decided to try a change of plan.

'No, there's no bleedin' proof about that.' He paused for a moment before asking, 'What are you going to do about my van then? I want her arrested for criminal damage, she's booted it at least twice.' I looked down at the offside panels of his battered van.

'Almost every panel is dented,' I pointed out. 'And most of these dents are already rusty, looks like old damage to me, which dents has she caused?'

'How the hell should I know?' He threw his arms up in despair. He was shouting. 'I was sat in the bleedin' van. I wasn't going to risk getting out with that mad bitch on the warpath.'

I don't know about him sitting in the van, hiding in the van would be more accurate. 'So there's no evidence about that either,' I asked. 'Now that's such a shame isn't it.'

'What?' he exclaimed. 'You mean you're not going to do owt about it?'

Now it was my turn to gloat, 'Well I'm sure that you'll understand, if there's no evidence that an offence has taken place then there's nothing I can do about it.'

He glared at me with a look of disgust, 'You're enjoying this aren't you, it's your way of getting your own back int it?'

'Yeah, that's right,' I replied. 'Quite funny really when you think about it? Now I suggest that you move your van so that these good people can use the car park, or you won't make any money at all today.'

On climbing into his van he slammed the door in anger. He sat in the driving seat for a moment or two, obviously not in a hurry to move. Over at Ruth's car I spoke to her through the open window, informed her that I'd just told Slade to move his van. She waited a few more seconds before losing patience with him. Then leaning her head out of the car window she bellowed, 'Oy, you, dick 'ed, move your effing van now, or I'll ram you out of the way.'

There was little doubt that she was prepared to do just that, it may even be worth watching! Slade obviously shared my opinion. He had now completely lost his nerve, he slammed his van into reverse gear and sped backwards. I thanked him with a sarcastic wave of the hand before stepping into the gap and waving Ruth through, happy to see her drive away. Slade sat in his van seething with anger and looking like the cowardly fool which he really was.

Minutes later I drove away congratulating myself on a successful outcome. Later I thought back to Mrs Crawford, she would be halfway back to York by now, but how I wish she could have been here to meet 'Roof from 'Alifax'. She would have enjoyed seeing how this incident played out. A bit of summary justice perhaps and the satisfaction of knowing that sometimes what goes around comes around!

Epilogue

Late in the afternoon I returned to the police station. I parked the car and made my way upstairs to the admin department, a part of the building I rarely visit. Jason, the civilian duties clerk, was waiting for our prearranged appointment. A part of his job was to update all the records and work out each officer's entitlement of annual leave and rest days. That was the information that I needed. In three months time I would reach my fiftieth birthday, the earliest date that I would be eligible for retirement. I wanted to know exactly when I could hand in my uniform, and it wasn't quite as straightforward as it may sound. To arrive at the relevant date Jason would need to add up all the rest days and annual leave that I had accrued over many years.

I sat alongside him as he went through the computer records. First he counted up the overtime I had worked without payment, added to that were cancelled rest days when I gave evidence at court. Within minutes he came up with a grand total of sixty-five days.

I peered over his shoulder at the screen and made a quick calculation, it looked promising. 'Right then,' I asked, 'if we count back from my fiftieth birthday, for sixty-five days when would I finish?' He worked his way through the calendar on his desk. Then he diligently double checked his calculations making sure that it was done correctly.

'According to my calculations, your last working day would be the day after tomorrow,' he announced.

I was astounded. 'The day after tomorrow?'

'Yes, I've checked it twice, definitely the day after tomorrow,' he said.

'That's fantastic Jason. Well if I can retire in two days' time then that's exactly what I'm going to do.'

I could hardly believe it. In only two days' time I would retire after twenty-six years as a copper. Time to live the dream, travel, seek adventure and explore the distant corners of the world. I was in good health, enough money in the bank and now I had the time too, what more could I ask. Of course all that was before I fell off my bike ... but that really is another story ...